FOOTBALL WITH
ATT*i*TUDE

STEVE REDHEAD

Photographs by Richard Davis

WORD SMITH

British Library Cataloguing-in-Publication Data
A catalogue record for this book is
available from the British Library

ISBN 1 873205 04 X

First published 1991
WORDSMITH, Progress Centre, Charlton Place,
Ardwick Green, Manchester M12 6HS.

Design and production: WORDSMITH

Cover design: Tandem Design & Illustration,
23 New Mount Street, Manchester M4 4DE.

Print: Manchester Free Press, Paragon Mill,
Jersey Street, Manchester M4 6FP

To Ruth, Laura and Eleanor
and my mother and father

acknowledgements

Many thanks to Ruth Redhead, Guy Lovelady, Richard Davis, Niall Allsop, Freya Rodger, Adrian Sherwood, Steve Barker, Fenny, Alan Haughton, Nikos Michas, Toni Melechi, Richard Haynes, Sarah Champion, Alison Martin, Eugene McLaughlin, Cor Gout, Derek Wynne, Mark Aherne, Kevin Cummins, Justin O'Connor, Ian Taylor, Andrew Ward, John Bale, Dennis Marsh, Steve Beauchampe, John Dewhirst, John Tummon, Attila The Stockbroker, Martin Thorpe, Steve Weatherill, Neil Duxbury, Pete Naylor, Gordon Taylor and anyone else who helped.

Thanks also to The Smiths for inspiration with the title of Chapter 1.

Thanks, especially, to all the fanzine editors who donated free copies of their fanzine to our archive and to the fans and faces who agreed to have their picture taken.

"That wasn't football, that was music"

Legendary Brazilian footballer, Péle, after
witnessing, in Italy, an outstanding Marco Van
Basten goal for AC Milan.
Reported in *The Guardian* (October 9 1990)

contents

sweet and tender hooligan
frankly mr shankly

Football has long been more than a game. When Bill Shankly (subject of 35 Summers' T-shirt design and, maybe, even The Smiths' **Frankly Mr Shankly**), Liverpool's legendary manager, claimed that soccer was far more important than life or death it was an understatement and not, as many outside soccer's goldfish-bowl thought it to be, an exaggeration. For most of the 80s professional football, in England and Wales in particular, was frequently said to be in irreversible decline. Shankly's death itself was cruelly immortalised by Liverpool's many fierce rivals in taunting banners, graffiti and chants:

> "Who's that lying on the roadway
> Who's that lying on the floor
> It's Bill Shankly on his back
> And he's had an 'art attack
> And he won't be going to Wembley anymore."

If soccer and society are inextricably bound together (as Shankly indicated in his famous dictum) the savagery of such retorts was undoubtedly rooted in underlying social and class changes, long-term economic decline, regional aspiration, de-industrialisation, urban decay and racial tension. Football still mirrors, and is mirrored by, society. There are plenty of long-lasting images and memories from the 1984-85 British miners' strike but the football chant 'Here We Go, Here We Go, Here We Go' catches the mood missed by yards of documentary television footage; determined, defiant defence and 'Attack, Attack, Attack, Attack, Attack'. Both more in hope than expectation.

It is now more than 100 years since playing soccer for money was legalised in Britain and we are certainly light years from the late 40s when crowds of 60,000-plus turned out to watch run-of-the-mill league games. But even today the 'beautiful game' provokes extraordinary passions and commitments. In the early 80s, in the wake of the worst recession for 50 years, soccer styles, on and off the field, were once again a major focus of attention. As the recession of the early 90s bites deep into the social fabric of the Home Counties and beyond, the rebirth of English soccer spectatorship – after its nadir in 1985 – will be tested to the full under the microscopic global eye of the media, especially in the build-up to

OPPOSITE
Junior Evertonians
Goodison Park, May 91.

the 1994 World Cup, to be held in the USA, the land of the mediascape.

Football with Attitude is essentially a series of documents, visual and textual, about the nature of football fandom; styles of watching, participating in and consuming football as a cultural product in the late 20th century. But, in describing such contemporary change this book seeks to prise open the relationship between the seemingly impervious football world and the equally nightmarish (though fascinating and seductive) hyperreal circus which goes on unceasingly outside the soccer stadia and the training ground.

There are plenty of football books telling us what Kenny Dalglish had for breakfast when he was a toddler or, at the other extreme, why (mostly) young, working class males like to kick the shit out of each other on a Saturday. But few, if any, recognise that there might be a connection between these behaviours.

My particular contribution to the pile of The-Sun-Soccer-Annual-in-summer-sale-baskets, **Sing When You're Winning**, was originally subtitled 'The Last Football Book', not because I didn't want to read (or write) any more but because the genre, like many aspects of the world game of soccer itself, became a gross parody of the plentiful meanings of football as a spectacle for those who watch and play it.

A second-hand bookshop list of "books about football" contains a bizarre reference to one of Leonard Gribble's books: **They Kidnapped Stanley Matthews: A Case For Superintendent Anthony Slade** (Jenkins 1950). I never did get hold of a copy but it struck me that, as Jimmy Greaves once lamented about playing the professional game in the 60s, a certain element of fun had gone out of football writing. From the mid-80s the football fanzine explosion – what may be labelled the 'new football writing' and is much of the focus of this book – soon put paid to that failing with dollops of parody, irony, satire, black humour and sometimes libellous comment. The editors of a Brighton and Hove Albion fanzine, **Gull's Eye**, were successfully sued by the club's directors and had to fork out £6,000, a sum eventually found with help from support campaigns.

For my part, I have followed the line of Leonard Gribble and taken much of what is presented in the media as 'soccer industry fact' with a lorry-load of salt. The trouble is that if I had ever been able to look inside Gribble's "fine copy in dust wrappers (torn at lower edge)" I would probably have found, like Jimmy Greaves if he were really honest, that English soccer style in the 50s was more toiling than triumphant; plenty of 'stopper' centre-halves as well as the odd teasing winger.

You can't always judge a book by looking at the cover (or title) and football's after-the-event notices are notoriously starry-eyed. Indeed, a theme of this book is precisely that football fan culture is massively influenced by the past century of professional soccer as part of popular culture and that our memories about that history which, even had we been there, are always mediated, never direct. Nostalgia in football, a yearning for a Golden Age when fans were peaceful and players were skilled yet obedient servants, is pervasive whether it be in the sports pages, the texts of official reports or commentaries by television's talking heads.

Such specific forms of nostalgia are often seen by cultural critics as part of a more general 'postmodern condition'; as if today's cultural products (films, novels, plays, music videos) can only function by plundering and parodying the past. But even if this were the case, that does not mean to say either that such a cultural fault-line always has to be seen negatively or that it does not contain many other significant features.

By using flashbacks woven into a series of fragmentary narratives (often based on my own interviews with players, directors, officials, Government ministers and, most of all, supporters) of the 'modern' era since England's 1966 World Cup win, **Football with Attitude** traces the conditions which produced the 'moment' of the football fanzine and the Football Supporters Association (FSA). It freeze-frames the creation of an active, democratic, participatory culture around soccer spectatorship in the late 20th century which has an integral connection to other contemporary aspects of youth and pop culture.

The aims of the F.S.A. are:

i ! to gain representation for supporters on the executive bodies which cont the game.

ii ! to provide a democratic organisatio which expresses the concerns of football supporters.

iii ! to promote goodwill between sup nationally and internationally, an foster the game of football.

THE FOOTBALL SUPPORTERS ASSOCIATION

One noteworthy link between modern cultural industries, such as football and popular music, is that both are as much about play as about work. The most common joint response emerging from contemporary interviews with professional football players and musicians, producers and DJs was that their current labour was not work: someday soon, if they were unfortunate, they would have to look for a 'real' job! Overall, **Football with Attitude** looks behind the glib notions of 'football madness', 'football crazy' (as one popular song of the 50s had it) and 'football mania'. It specifies, more accurately than ghosted autobiographies and dense, learned academic treatises, why football as popular culture is a source of such multiple pleasures for its millions of 'fans'; that is, players, administrators and spectators alike. It cheerfully dissects the nostalgia for a 'lost' Golden Age and captures the flavour of the rapid changes in football fan culture from the demise of the maximum wage in the early 60s to the 90s, incorporating both the savoury and unsavoury.

The latter are inseparable. More often than not witty terrace chants are created and sung by the very 'lads' who are willing to fight running street-battles or scrap in a 'known' pub before and after the match: 'Sing Your Hearts Out For The Lads' and other spectator anthems of the 90s rapidly degenerate into sexual, racial or political abuse. Equally the most skilful and entertaining players are frequently identified as troublemakers within the industry and are most often subjected to disciplinary regulation or media pillory – Paul Gascoigne is one such emblem for the early 90s. There are no pure elements of football pleasure: joy and strife are two dimensions of the same coin. Further, mass media concentration on 'hooliganism' on the one hand and what top professional players get paid on the other has obscured the thousands of under-rewarded club 'servants' (a very appropriate football phrase) and the hundreds of thousands of fans (often of clubs outside the élite) for whom the products of the professional soccer industry, however perverse it may seem, are simply addictive.

And now … a story about a story. My first stab at a narrative of events in the English football industry of the late 70s and mid-80s emerged as **Sing When You're Winning: The Last Football Book**. Written in 1985 (the year of Heysel and Bradford) and eventually published by Pluto Press in 1987, its format and title were a parody of a particular mode of popular media-writing familiar around the time of the origins of the punk youth subculture in 1976-77. (This style was best exemplified by Julie Burchill and Tony Parsons in **The Boy Looked At Johnny: The Obituary of Rock and Rolls**.) The figures of compulsive punning, stream of consciousness 'speed'-writing, anarchic plunder of popular songs and chants and the deliberate over-the-top trashing of received orthodoxies and personae permeated both titles. **Sing When You're Winning**'s account of football culture was designed as a pastiche of a pop culture style which had already lost its radical, subversive edge when applied to popular cultural forms (such as pop music, fashion and youth culture) and was just beginning to be used to describe the decaying relationship between the football industry and its long-suffering consumers. **The Absolute Game**, the general Scottish football fanzine was, to my knowledge, the only publication to identify the source of my inspiration but missed the intended irony. **The Scotsman** contained a review of the book by Robbie Dinwoodie which rightly pinpointed it as the "first postmodernist book on the place of football" in English popular culture while football fans in the music industry recognised its pioneering forays into the tangled web of soccer's political and cultural connection to popular music. DJ John Peel praised it on Radio 1, wireless colleague and DJ Steve Barker gave over an hour to it on Radio Lancashire's **On The Wire** and ace mixologist Adrian Sherwood named it as his favourite book in an **NME** feature. The publishers chose to adorn it with the legend, or myth, "a post-punk book on football" ("post-punk junk" as one fanzine sniped!) and I suppose that was a reasonably accurate epigram, though I personally prefer "amusing and anarchic" which another reviewer coined.

The intended focus of **Sing When You're Winning**, then, were those who consumed football as a popular cultural product. These consumers were generally the regular supporters who were, and indeed are,

frequently treated to the most appalling conditions (including, in many cases, the spectacle on the field) for their entrance money plus, increasingly, a membership fee. Yet for 20 or 30 years these same spectators have been consistently marked out in the media – by officials, Government ministers, police chiefs, as well as journalists – as possible, or actual, criminals; as predictably violent delinquents rather than the consumer audience which remains (despite attempts to make it otherwise) the lifeblood of a modern leisure industry with a potentially mammoth global pulling-power.

Pluto Press' chosen cover, Eamonn McCabe's superb 80s shot of angry young men chasing after a rapidly fleeing opponent, achieved the predictable outcome. Given the context of the widespread post-Heysel 'law and order' rhetoric, I was (and still am) plagued by journalists and television companies wanting to know where they could record for posterity a piece of the football (hooligan) action or, in some cases at least, simulate such practices for their readers or viewers.

The fact that the book was written deliberately and carefully to counter such an interpretation of professional football signifying violence and public disorder, mattered little. One national newspaper described it as a "cynical, twisted and tasteless view of Heysel" as if I had invented chants such as 'Heysel, Heysel '85' rather than simply reported them, though another did perceive the real intentions behind the writing to be an "idiosyncratic look at the terrible ills that threaten the beautiful game." In one regional newspaper interview where I had given an account of the football fanzine collection, built up in the wake of researching the book, someone selected the singularly inappropriate banner headline of "The Carnage Yet To Come For Football" for an article on fan magazines which are overwhelmingly committed to non-violence.

I was even taken to task in another forum for celebrating football casual terrace crews as the new "shock troops of revolution"! On the other hand **Socialist Worker** called it an "attractively laid out pile of style" in which, it said, "the politics are bankrupt". The book, as Albert Hunt noted in his passionate **New Society** review, was certainly savage, and there was additionally an unleashing of anger both at the seeming imminent death of a part of social life and the crass reporting and presentation of football fan culture in the global media. Nothing much had changed. As another reviewer of **Sing When You're Winning** put it, the book was manifestly a "supreme child of its times" and an "ideal candidate for a place in a time capsule". Nevertheless, in many ways we are still in those "times".

There are certainly reasons to be more cautiously optimistic than I dared be in 1985. At that time I could count on the fingers of one hand the number of football fanzines. Mostly they were one club 'zines like Bradford City's **City Gent**, York City's **Terrace Talk**, Bolton Wanderers' **Wanderers Worldwide**. **When Saturday Comes** (in sale terms the most successful football fanzine) and **Off The Ball** (now sadly no more, deliberately unplugged when it was in its prime) were just beginning. The word 'fanzine' (literally an abbreviation of fan magazine) conjured up the popular music (mainly punk) fanzines of the mid-70s to early 80s. Football spectators were barely represented by traditional, and often conservative, supporters clubs and their national federation, not yet the emerging FSA which I, like thousands of others, soon joined. Surrealist inflatable crazes and joyful terrace croons like Man City's revival of the 1934 Rodgers and Hart classic **Blue Moon** seemed centuries away in the wake of the Heysel and Valley Parade stadia tragedies. The football/indie/dance crossover which took off globally in the late 80s and early 90s was very much in its infancy; The Farm, for instance, were then the 'house' band of Merseyside's cult music/football fanzine, **The End**.

Football With Attitude seeks to preserve **Sing When You're Winning**'s "savage entertainment" (as one reviewer put it) within a format which strives for, "more than a scoreless draw of a book – more like 4-4 after 90 minutes with a penalty shoot out to come" (as another had it) and in **City Gent**'s words, a feeling that you are being forced to engage in a "never-ending pub conversation" about a particular object of desire in popular culture.

Cheers!

The new FOOTBALL man

where are you now, georgie?

Professional soccer is, strange as it may seem, part of what was long ago described as "the culture industry". Unusually for a cultural industry though, football – and footballers – have not exactly been the epitome of style, and in a supposedly style-obsessed decade like the 80s that was bad news.

In the 60s George Best (the "Belfast Boy", as Don Fardon put it) was an exception rather than the rule, as it turned out. Without succumbing to a shred of nostalgia it is possible to assert that no amount of Brut advertising could give the Gazza (one of the "Geordie Boys", as Paul Gascoigne sang it on the cash-in album **Let's Have A Party**) media phenomenon the same potency or lasting charisma. The last (and first) person to give Margaret Thatcher a hug on television may be an appropriate epitaph; or the man who eventually resurrected Lindisfarne with their 90s chart hit remake **Fog On The Tyne (Revisited)**. Meanwhile an on-field photograph of George Best – 60s 'El Beatle' style – adorned The Wedding Present's first independent chart album, also named after the Man United star. The now defunct popular music magazine **Jamming!** described Best – a few years before appearing drunk and disorderly on **Wogan** – as:

> "one of those incomparable individuals – a timely opportune genius. A sixties child. If anything, George Best was style pure and simple. Furthermore, like ... great stylists he found his place in time and created his own legend."

In the late 80s a diverse sport and music crossover crew, including post-punk football fans such as John Robb of The Membranes and Sensurround and former editor of mid-80s fanzine, **The Rox**, plus assorted members of The Three Johns, The Mekons and Chumbawamba, combined as Sportchestra!. On **101 Songs About Sport** (Agit-Prop) they played a more affectionate lament for the Best:

> "Where are you now Georgie?
> With those boots that laced up the side
> And that Irish shirt that you wore with pride
> And that picture of you with Mike Summerbee and bride
>
> Where are you now Georgie?
> I dreamed of you dribbling past City's back four
> And leaving Joe Corrigan fumbling on the floor

OPPOSITE
Everton's Pat Nevin with **Is It Red** seller Goodison Park, May 91.

15

And the Stretford End singing 'More Bestie! More!'

Where are you now Georgie?
In a boutique down Carnaby Street
Or gambling on the horses at an Aintree meet
Oh where oh where are those magic feet?

I know where you've been -
On Granada every week
I want you to come back to me!
And have you seen George Oghani
And Charlie George?"

However, since Best's heyday players have rarely had the right haircut. Moreover, the media fascination with the game's origins in long shorts, big boots and flat caps has turned historical memory into a millstone around soccer's neck.

But there are new club cultures emerging from beneath the wooden stands, crumbling terraces and steaming Bovril. The **New Musical Express** (NME) once described Chelsea, Everton and Scotland's small, stylish winger, Pat Nevin, as a "post-punk" footballer, referring as much to his musical tastes as his natty line in crosses and goal scoring. Yet there is much more permanent substance than such a label might imply. Nevin, among other characteristics in the make-up of 'The Thinking Fan's Footballer', has been outspoken against racism in football and supported both soccer fanzines and the FSA.

In youth culture, the birth of the casuals on soccer terraces gave a new dimension to sportswear and menswear and fixed a notion of a crossover between football and dance clubs which was to long outlive this particular development in youth culture. In addition, despite notices of its impending demise for most of the 80s, professional football is, along with popular music, a key leisure industry serving the ever more variegated youth market. The players are themselves between 17 and 35 years old. Even younger age groups are often the basis of many teams' home, and even travelling, support; not to mention the vast pool of young telly addicts ripe for the merchandising of football and other products.

From 1985 what captured the imagination of thousands of football fans (of both sexes) in their teens, 20s and 30s was the explosion of football fanzines exploiting the accessibility of desktop technology and constituting

Foreword by Kevin Keegan

an excess of print addiction to rival the rush of independent record labels and music fanzines in the wake of punk in the 70s. The undoubted success story of independent publishing was acknowledged in May 1991 by the Birmingham Readers and Writers Festival which held a day-long event, 'You'll Never Read Alone', a dissection of football writing which incorporated the first ever National Awards for Football Fanzines.

Furthermore, there was the closely connected birth and rise of the first 'alternative' organisation of football spectators – namely the FSA. This helped constitute a new 'democracy' movement dedicated to increasing spectator participation at various levels of the game. The movement also fostered a more rational and humanitarian outlook in a football world which had exhibited the horrors of Bradford, Heysel and Hillsborough in just five short years.

Much of the soccer industry seems mercilessly manipulative. Flair, skill and fun are frequently squeezed out of the spectacle in the relentless search for precious points to stave off relegation. The clichés ('over the (blue) moon', 'sick as a parrot', 'well Jimmy', 'take each game as it comes', 'at the end of the day') are churned out for the press, television and radio almost as fast as local businessmen join the board for quick publicity and a few free tickets.

But by the late 80s and early 90s, individual and team styles showed some signs of staging a fightback. Occasionally among the flying boots in a 20yd strip either side of the halfway line there are glimpses of football's 'magic' – the spontaneous excitement generated by a great goal, a defence-splitting pass, the 'best save since Gordon Banks from Péle', or merely the biting wit of 10,000 terrace wags which finds its way unedited to the armchair audience's ears. Those who think this is pure revivalism – a replay of the ghost of football past – should think again. Whatever the massed ranks of media pundits might say, Paul Gascoigne, John Barnes, Gary Lineker, Chris Waddle and Peter Beardsley are not new George Bests; not because their various, diverse skills don't compare but because this is not a re-run of the 60s, or for that matter the 50s, 40s or 1890s.

There is a wider significance now attached to winning the battles of soccer politics, either on or off the field, which differs markedly from those which have gone before.

In one of the few books to capture the flavour of the football culture of its period (albeit one which had disappeared by the time of its first publication in 1968) The Football Man: People and Passions in Soccer, journalist and dramatist Arthur Hopcraft wrote:

> "Football crowds are never going to sound or look like the hat parade on the club lawns of Cheltenham racecourse. They are always going to have more vinegar than Chanel".

However, the 70s and 80s made Hopcraft's confident late-60s pronouncement look a little tattered.

Today's football industry is marketing its product for different types of consumer, what the former players' union leader, Jimmy Hill, described as a "non-hooligan" audience. Hill's own flamboyant solution (underlined by Lord Justice Taylor in his influential Report after the Hillsborough disaster), which was much hawked around the boardrooms when he was Managing Director of Coventry City, was to install an all-seater stadium, the first of its kind in the English league. The Highfield Road experiment went badly wrong: a few away supporters wrecked it (the seats proved much more difficult to police) and home supporters protested in no uncertain manner that they had a right to stand on the terraces. These arguments were raised again more generally when the Government announced its plans to accept parts of the Taylor Report and implement all-seater stadia for sports grounds by the end of the century ... and then received a House of Commons Home Affairs Committee paper on 'Policing Football Hooliganism' which, in supporting many other FSA recommendations, suggested only a minority of grounds should be without terraces. 'You're not standing anymore', anyone?

However, it is easier said than done to draw the Young Fogies, New Georgians, Sloane Rangers and the rest of the social-climbing fraternity to an involvement with the football industry in sufficient numbers to displace the proletarian hordes. Soccer is an unlikely sport for young aspiring professionals and they are more likely to buy up football clubs than flock to the grounds as paying spectators. Nonetheless the bedrock of traditional football support, the skilled and white-collar, white, male worker, has drifted away from the turnstiles in large enough numbers to make the industry's marketing strategy target a richer and less restricted audience.

If professional soccer in England and Wales is still in some way a 'working class sport', if it deserves the romanticised epithet 'the people's game', it can be partly sensed in its connection to popular music, youth and fashion. In 80s-speak, this was thought to be about 'style'. As The Face, the London-based youth culture magazine most responsible for introducing the politics of style into the recession-devastated early 80s, put it in its self-designated "fifth anniversary party" in 1985:

> "Style has become the most persistent cliché and the most powerful currency of our times. In the visual age the look is what really counts ... but this heightened and even more hedonistic new mod sensibility has taken hold against the backdrop of an economy garrotted by Thatcherism".

The Face view that the "hero of our times is simply a thief in the right training shoes" became a complex emblem for an age in which, on American mean streets at least, youths have been murdered for their designer footwear and jackets. In the mid-80s when Robert Elms coined the phrase it denoted a whole footballing following which is, in many senses, still the basis for clubs 'on tour'. As Jimmy Corkhill, a character in Merseyside's television soap opera, Brookside, snipes: "this world's full of thieves and scallies".

Trainers, in the football industry, have long meant specific varieties of Puma and Adidas rather than a middle-aged man without much puff running onto the field carrying the magic sponge. The emergence in the late 70s and early 80s of scallies, perries and chaps made football grounds, nightclubs and shopping malls a veritable catwalk for designer labels at a time when the English game (and the British nation) was being widely condemned as bankrupt and virtually dead.

nce the exclusive domai
confessed 'headers', Leeds
terraces have been invaded b
breed of hedonistic supporte
United fans were kicking more
sand castles down in Bour
irts bearing the sinister motto "Nob
on't Care". This season, evidently fe
a third Summer of Love, the Ell
claring "Peace, Love and United"
adge of the Seventies has been re
of harmony, sincere or otherwise,
hink there's something sardonic abo
alking round
'peace' and
acks," says
Moose. "It
e football's
em, but at
a lot better
s and ski-
ybe people
t the mes-
Marcus

Jnited" T-shirts
uffalo, 66 New
AV, 9-11 Trinity
le Leeds United
and Road, price
hort- and long-
ectively

The dole queue has always beckoned football fans, especially in the period between the wars, but rarely have they celebrated it with such flash and arrogant defiance. Young fans in the last 15 years have made travelling to, watching and travelling back from matches places to be seen and not just heard (or, more appropriately in view of what has become standard policing practice, herded). Kevin Sampson, writer for, among others, **The End** and manager of The Farm, described for **The Face** readers – in an article which the magazine sidelined for 18 months – how, by 1981:

> "just about every team in the country was able to boast a collection of match-dudes, each trying to outdo the next city in terms of terrace cool ... I maintain that there are few finer moments in life than when you step into an alien city en masse, all dressed up ruthless, and watch those people stare."

Whatever football traditions say about its down-market origins, soccer and style fanatics said it loud and clear that the way we wear is more important than the way we were. But where did this obsession with football fashion spring from? What forced this desire to look good on match days as well as **The Match**? This dedicated following of style league table fashion has complex roots, reflecting and inflaming regional, ethnic and social rivalries.

These tensions surfaced in brutal and cruel form during the year-long British miners' strike of 1984-85 leaving Yorkshire teams, like Sheffield Wednesday and Leeds United, firmly identified, in the minds of other teams' fans, with Arthur Scargill's line on the dispute, "Arthur Scargill, is a wanker, is a wanker" they sang, not to mention, "You only wish you were mining".

Chants from fans at matches between these teams and clubs from so-called 'moderate' areas like Nottinghamshire and Lancashire were increasingly vitriolic even beyond the official end of the dispute and a favourite reciprocatory taunt was "You scab bastards, you scab bastards". Some teams' fans remake of the Liverpool Kop's mid-60s anthem **You'll Never Walk Alone** had regularly become 'You'll Never Walk Again' by the 70s:

> "Sign on, sign on

> With hope in your hearts
> And you'll never get a job"

along with "One job between you, you've only got one job between you" as an alternative to 'Sing when you're winning' to the tune of **Guantanamera**, and 'Get to work you lazy twats' when sung in the mid-80s constituted the sequel to Alan Bleasdale's bleak burial of labourism in **Boys From The Blackstuff**, a television series which even featured, in one episode, Liverpool players Sammy Lee and Graeme Souness:

> "He's only a poor little scouser
> His face all tattered and torn
> He made me feel sick so I hit him with a brick
> And now he don't sing anymore."

and,

> "In your Liverpool slums
> You look in the dustbin for something to eat
> You find a dead rat and think it's a treat
> In your Liverpool slums."

continue to be evergreens in the terrace choirs' repertoire, with variations depending on who is singing to whom. When sung by Man City and United fans to Everton and Liverpool supporters it turned up a ratchet the already bitter rivalry between Manchester and Merseyside. This rivalry produced banners and graffiti proclaiming 'Munich 58' in reply to 'Shankly 81' as a cynical reminder of the tragic air crash in 1958 which decimated the Busby Babes and England through the loss of many great individual players.

The same taunts came from London fans – especially around the time of the miners' strike – flashing fivers and tenners in front of the tube trains when Merseyside boys were back in town, in a mimicry of the Metropolitan Police, as legend has it, on the northern picket lines during the coal dispute. But it is not just local Derbies – much-beloved of ecstatic television commentators until the trouble starts – that underlay the headlong plunge to wear it well or at least better than anybody else.

Traditional North-South divides, unevenly distributed in reality but palpably sharpened by long-term economic decline, have been stretched and bent to include nationalist and religious dimensions. For example, the proliferation of Celtic ski-hats in the

OPPOSITE
Liverpool fans
Anfield gates, May 91.

North West in the 1984-85 season followed the Glasgow club's visits to Old Trafford for a testimonial match for Lou Macari (former player with Celtic and Man United) and the much-publicised replayed match against Rapid Vienna in the European Cup Winners' Cup. Two-dimensional ski-hats, naming different clubs on each side of the head, soon became a compulsory purchase by thousands of parents for their children but, as a letter to a national newspaper at the time keenly observed, there was a significant link between Celtic, the casuals and the colours:

> "A few years ago the wearing of scarves became uncool among the 'scallies' and others who formed the backbone of away support. Then about four years ago it became acceptable to wear colours for Derby games, with bobble hats the most popular item. They really took off towards the end of last season (1983-84). With the scallies' propensity to be different, the progression to Celtic and Rangers was natural. But as with all trends it quickly caught on. Now the trick is to come up with the most unusual bobble hat. At Liverpool games we now see Juventus, German teams, some smarties even wearing Aberdeen or Hearts hats".

It might be comforting for those who still believe in the media stereotype of lovable-Scousers-singing-Beatles-songs-on-the-Kop to argue that this is simply another variation of soccer's style wars. Although such fads are, to some extent, market-based – "its because they sell them and they are different" – the Catholic symbolism of clubs such as Everton, Man United and Celtic is still strong, without reaching the depths of Rangers' trenchant Protestant sectarianism which the signing of Mo Johnston, a Catholic and former Celtic favourite, has not completely effaced. The flying of Irish tricolours, among other flags, is not entirely innocent or unconnected to style warfare and the geographical regrouping (until England vs Scotland matches) of northern English and Scottish fans against the rest is certainly part of a stylistic contempt for the self-labelled, trend-setting, fashionable teams from London.

The scallies' move away from casual to scruffy-look in the mid-80s was both a reflection of relative economic and social circumstances in the region and a burning desire to keep one step ahead of a style

latched onto elsewhere. Where trends start, or who is ahead in the style draws division in which month, is of course a matter of fierce debate. As Kevin Sampson argued in **The Face**, though, the origins of casual style can be traced fairly accurately, if without definitive resolution:

> "It was around February of 1978 that this fledgling fashion shook off its punk influences and became more of a cult, a football orientated lifestyle ... Though drinking, stealing, claiming and clubbing were all important, obsession with clothes gripped young Merseyside something murderous ... The beginning of the 1979 football season saw the Liverpool look popularised to a national level. Manchester with its 'Perries' and London's "Chaps" quickly imitated and emulated their scouse rivals by the sheer range of selection and the class of their clothing".

Whether it was flares (trousers not smoke bombs), ski-hats, sports or menswear, mountain gear or fancy dress; whether it was bought, looted, or bought with the proceeds of looting; wherever the location responsible for what the rest of the nation does tomorrow, the rise and rise of the casuals remained a wicked caricature of the supposedly affluent, "85% have-never-had-it-so-good" 80s. How ironic that it was football stadia that saw the development of the flashiest rag trade story since Carnaby Street while many of football's bosses and their masters and mistresses in government reacted to the crisis in manufacturing industry like a card school on the Titanic. In a nation where Margaret Thatcher, as Prime Minister, barely ventured out of the south east of England, unless it was to travel abroad, soccer's style wars became more important, and more vicious, than its multifarious Star Wars conducted in the transfer market, television studios and tabloid back pages. They took on a new significance beyond being a focus for this week's model and football fad leagues.

The economic crisis of the early 80s hit professional football as hard as it hit the staple industry of its traditional major heartlands. Initially, the early 80s 'shake-out' of firms massively reduced the number of spectators prepared, or able, to go and watch professional soccer matches (further accelerating a post-war historical trend until the late 80s) and decimated much of the football industry's workforce. Style in this context became more than what pop and cultural critic, Simon Frith, has called "bullying clothed in respectability", though it is often precisely that; it is inextricably bound up with what might be called a postmodern reaction to the death of the modern game.

If, symbolically not actually, the death of modern English football occurred around the mid-80s, the modern era can be seen to begin about1966, shortly after the end of the maximum wage system which limited the earnings of soccer players before 1961 and the celebrated court case of 1963 when Arsenal's George Eastham took his former club, Newcastle United, to the High Court to win a declaration that the old retain and transfer system was illegal. Though these twin bonds of what was seen in some quarters as soccer slavery were substantially broken, the "football revolution", as one Law Professor saw it, was not quite the watershed that was claimed for it in the 60s when Johnny Haynes of Fulham became the first Football League player to be paid £100 per week and players began to have more choice over whom they worked and played for.

England's1966 World Cup win, under the full glare of the publicity of Marshall McLuhan's global village, meant that the English version of the beautiful game received a massive new boost, internationally as well as nationally. Nevertheless, the transfer system, the chattel market of contemporary soccer, lived on despite the efforts of the the Professional Footballers Association (PFA) to get it fundamentally changed. Master and servant still, rather than employer and employee.

However incompletely, the chains of a 'traditional' professional football system of industrial relations were broken in the early 60s to produce the modern game: short shorts, lightweight boots and (seemingly) money to burn. The much-longed-for freedom of contract (players remaining free agents at the end of their contracts with whatever club) was won by 1978. But numerous battles to get a European-style multiplier compensation system accepted (based on age, previous experience, status of previous club,

and salary) have failed miserably. PFA warnings of the collapse of the domestic football industry without such a reform have constantly fallen on deaf ears. The big transfer market crash, with the consequent loss of confidence at the banks (players are assets after all, in many cases virtually the only assets) came at the beginning of the 80s.

By 1981 it was being confidently predicted that the days of £1 million-plus transfer deals were numbered – at least at home – but such, now common, (even paltry in the age of multi-million pound arrangements for the likes of Roberto Baggio in his transfer from Fiorentina to Juventus in 1990), seven-figure sums had only started changing grubby hands in the late 70s. These were often on hire-purchase or staggered terms, effectively meaning that few were actually paid in full.

The collapse of transfer values, occurring as it did almost overnight in the 1980-81 season, led directly to clubs, suddenly denied the revenue from the summer and winter sales, cutting costs drastically. The result: redundancies, severe wage cuts and ever-increasing reliance on part-time, Youth Training Scheme and, latterly, Enterprise Allowance Scheme players. The crash of Bristol City Football Club acted as a warning sign and the PFA's fight for compensation for breach of players' contracts of employment became a *cause célèbre:* the case of the "Bristol City Eight" as campaigning journalist, Peter Ball, dubbed the sacked players. As Julie Welch, with Cynthia Bateman a rare token woman in a (to sample James Brown) "man's man's man's" game, stated at the time, the club was put:

> "on the verge of extinction and eight loyal players in a horrible dilemma ... Geoff Merrick, Chris Garland, Jimmy Mann, David Rodgers, Peter Aitken, Gerry Sweeney, Julian Marshall and Trevor Tainton had contracts worth £290,000; Bristol City, once in the First Division but now in the Third had debts of £1.5 million and assets of £78,000 plus their ground".

Since the winter of 1982 when Bristol City (as was) went down there have been a string of clubs rushing towards (and in some cases over) the precipice – Hereford United, Derby County, Aldershot, Newport

County, Bradford City, Wigan Athletic, Tranmere Rovers, Wolverhampton Wanderers and Middlesbrough – though few 'Ashton Gate Eights' who eventually received good PFA-secured redundancy terms.

In the intervening years inflated transfer fees, the pervasive activities of agents and rocketing salaries for an élite of top players all played their part in the appearance of a (footballing) economic miracle. Everything in the garden looked rosy again; moreover arts and cultural industries (which embraced football, however awkwardly) were seen widely as means of economic regeneration. Then the Hillsborough disaster took place.

The recession which has blighted the world economy – but especially Britain's – in the early 90s threatens to inflict even more concerted damage on a football industry already reeling from the Taylor Report. Its recommendations on all-seater stadia undermine the very existence of dozens of clubs, which, despite the provision of funds through the Football Trust, legitimately cry "can't pay, won't pay" poll-tax style.

This is the economic context of a renewal of 'style' in professional football in the present: another national industry, a curious symbol of Britain's great manufacturing and imperial past, teetering on the brink, by its very continued existence in the form of almost a hundred professional league clubs (and hundreds more well-organised and economically viable in non-league soccer) defying the economic logic of politicians of the New Right. By the mid-80s the 'modernists', such as there were, appeared in retreat. The modern game, in all its facets, was getting its comeuppance with a vengeance and there was a sneaking suspicion that traditionalists as well as free market Conservatives were saying "I told you so". By the 80s, intricate short-passing games and cautious management had made everyone a workaholic midfielder, rather than the joyous, attacking, adventurous stylists of 'total' football envisaged by, for instance, Johan Cruyff's Dutch national team in the 70s. The 'new' football playing styles which emerged instead, like the long ball, kick-and-rush mode employed by various incarnations of Sheffield Wednesday, Wimbledon, Watford, Crystal Palace and Sheffield United in the 80s, were often perverse, exaggerated versions of earlier styles from football's long and varied past. Up-and-under tactics became more and more popular – frequently involving goalkeepers hoofing the pig's bladder onto the edge of the opponent's penalty area from yards outside their own box – primarily having the effect of missing out the congested midfield altogether. It still looks like something out of the 19th century before rugby separated from association football.

The fact that such anti-modernist styles in professional soccer were really pre-modern was significant. They harked back to the Good Old Days; that is, prior to the modern era, when men were men, gaffers were gaffers and the imported styles of the continent (European, or South American – it hardly mattered) with their emphasis on a prettier, less (or different) masculine form of play could be ignored more readily. The underhandedness of the 'dirty tricks' departments of Italian, Spanish, Argentinian and Uruguayan teams and the suspect political infections of the Eastern bloc sides (even after the fall of the Berlin Wall) were matched by good old English phlegm, or work rate as we have learned to know it on the football, rather than the battle, field. Pre-modern times in the nation's soccer were characterised by a cultural, colonial superiority born of the Empire and a physical toughness hewed out of hard but deferential labour.

The 60s and 70s sometimes brought what commentators saw as an 'effeminacy' to English football styles. Just think of Granada TV's 70s dynamic duo talk show **The Perfect Match** featuring Rodney Marsh and George Best repeated in the late 80s; or look again at Best's pose on The Wedding Present's **George Best** cover which was, to many commentators and critics, positively un-English or plain 'foreign'. Appropriately to such critics, Best, who played for Northern Ireland, and Marsh, who gained a mere handful of England caps, were both to spend the majority of the late 70s and 80s involved in an ailing North American soccer league rather than what is still misnamed 'the best League in the World'. The outright rejection by the English national team

management of the sweeper (or *libero*) system, apart from the later stages of the 1990 World Cup in Italy when it proved so successful, was based on similar grounds. The same goes for the very slow and extremely partial adoption of the sweeper (almost always in England, mistakenly, seen as a defensive ploy) in the higher echelons of the League – or even for that matter man-to-man marking as a strategy. 'Continental' was, in the last analysis, forever inferior to 'home' even when the evidence was overwhelmingly in the opposite direction.

All in all the impression was left that if the development of the modern game could somehow, with a great leap backwards, be put into reverse perhaps the Good Old Days would come again. Maybe if we dug far back into the history of the game (and the nation) we could come up with a few Victorian values (aesthetic **and** economic) even some new, untried, market remedies which might halt the decline of sport and of state.

Changes in Football League rules, allowing clubs to keep home gate receipts, did give precisely such a twist of economic liberalism to the traditional framework of English soccer in the mid-late 80s. As social historian of sport, Tony Mason, has pointed out:

> "Up to 1983-84 the League was a kind of cartel in which some income was redistributed from the better off to the poorer clubs. Home clubs paid a percentage of their gate to the visitors. Money from football pools, club competitions and television was shared out equally to clubs."

However, such distributive justice effectively ended for the 1983-84 season with the League's decision to make home teams keep the proceeds of their matches – just what Arsenal, Man United, Liverpool, Spurs and Everton (the so-called Big Five) ordered. A 'Super League' was effectively soon formed out of television appearance arrangements way before the FA revealed its plans to the Football League in 1991. The idea of poor clubs getting poorer and the rich clubs getting richer, along with the game's megastar managers and players sucking in astronomical salaries and other earners such as product endorsements and contracted tabloid columns (though substantially less than they could make in Europe), accorded very

neatly with the life and times of Britain in the grip of 'boot boy' economics. It also laid the ground for 'radical' solutions to alleviate the mess which was itself caused by the widening gap between those at the top and the many more at the bottom. To quote the braying voices on the right side of what used to be Fleet Street:

> "British football is in crisis: a slum sport played in slum stadiums and increasingly watched by slum people, who deter decent folk from turning up ... The game needs cleaning up and revitalising every bit as much as the rest of Victorian industrial Britain. Reassessment should start from the fairly obvious fact that it must stand or fall on its popularity. If people do not want to watch a match then there is no reason in the world why 22 men [sic] should be paid to play it. Football like any other professional entertainment, is nothing if it does not draw crowds on its merits. Subsidising entertainment is a contradiction in terms, for if it needs subsidising it surely cannot be very entertaining."

This aptly titled **Sunday Times** editorial "Putting The Boot In", written in the wake of the Bradford City fire disaster, is made all the harder to resist when football followers are bombarded (usually on the sports pages of the same papers) with the everyday images of the 'ungrateful', 'greedy' and 'overpaid' professional footballer who is bleeding the game to death in between getting out of bed with a collection of 'bimbos' and opening a boutique.

But this is far from the whole story. Players' monetary wages in professional soccer are notoriously overstated given the relative employment insecurity they suffer. For the vast majority of League professionals the financial rewards are comparatively meagre. Not bad, but then footballers have always been better off than many of those who watched them ... even in the 30s under the maximum wage. Signing on fees with, occasionally, in the case of big names, massive attendant television publicity, striking glamour poses and other less identifiable and taxable ways of getting in the readies, have long been a means of offsetting the risks and the short-term employment prospects.

At one time, especially after 1967 when the PFA negotiated a 10% transfer levy (half of which went to the Players' Provident Fund and the other half to the players themselves as long as they did not request the transfer), the professional players had a vested interest in escalating transfer fees. Inflation in the transfer market meant enormous benefits for some footballers in transit without the hassle of actually negotiating a figure for signing on – often the hardest and meanest bargaining in football's industrial relations jungle and one in which the increasing number of players' agents have played their hand with remarkable force.

Nevertheless, by the early 80s such inequalities were being curbed somewhat, following the PFA's successful claim for standardised footballers pension schemes giving players pension rights at 35, itself achieved only after years of struggle with the Football League and the Inland Revenue. Theoretically, pensions, funded by contributions or League levy on transfers, meant that the end of the 'famous international hits hard times' headlines, although the likes of Kevin Beattie (England and Ipswich Town) could testify otherwise.

Tommy Lawton (Chelsea, Everton, Notts County and England) was perhaps the best known of this genre, falling right over-the-moon-into-the-gutter after his playing days finished. He described this condition in one of football's more poignant autobiographies – usually pulp fiction – **When The Cheering Stopped: The Rise, The Fall**:

> "Football carried me to many interesting places, the Kremlin and the Vatican included ... Life outside the game saw me in the dole queue and the police court and I experienced the doubtful company of bailiffs and debt collectors."

The 5% of transfer fees going to players themselves was curtailed once the new pension scheme was implemented in the wake of the 1978 'freedom of contract' agreement so that old 'working class heroes' like Lawton would no longer have to sign on at another, less salubrious venue.

That did not, of course, prevent players negotiating signing on fees individually or receiving under-the-counter payments or even goods. The early 80s' economic recession put something of a brake on sums involved in such deals (many players were just glad

to have a job), but they gathered pace again towards the end of the decade.

Thus the football revolution, which was promised (and hailed) in the context of 1966 and all that, may have created the modern game but that modernism now looks pretty tawdry from the vantage point of the 90s. The "people's art", as Arthur Hopcraft once called it, is in need of radical renewal. To ask whether football is actually up or down (market) in the last decade of the 20th century is not the only, or even the best, gauge of its popularity. In many ways what matters is that it still exists in a recognisable form and, despite various ravages visited upon it, allows relatively cheap entertainment to be served up to a mass audience – whether, as in the past, at the ground or, increasingly, on live television.

The only other comparable cultural industry today is popular music, though both are, in different ways, locked into the incessant production and consumption of a 'global culture', a key feature of what cultural critics mean by postmodernism. The link between the two industries goes back to the late 19th century where both the origins of professional soccer and the music hall can be traced to a more generalised birth of popular culture between the 1880s and 1920s.

As part of The Culture Industry they have often been subjected, misguidedly, to the mass culture critique which criticises such low culture activities for their pervasive mass psychological effects on un-suspecting, and potentially revolting, citizens. Gerhard Vinnai's **Football Mania** (published in English in the early 70s with an astute introduction by David Triesman) was one such project, discussing the soccer business in terms more often reserved for the trashing of popular music as an 'art' form and as an ideological barrier to fully-fledged "revolutionary consciousness". Not that this partly negative view of pop and football is confined to those on the left. The New Right in philosophy has more recently condemned educationalists who fail to preserve the "heritage of classical music", thereby fudging the high/low culture divide between classical and 'rock' music. One professor argued:

> "I personally object to the teaching of rock music. It is barbaric and degrading. Music education has a

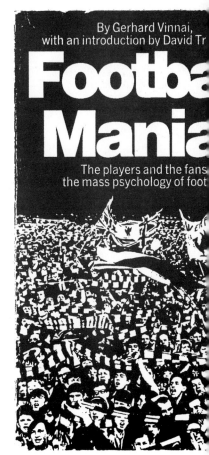

By Gerhard Vinnai, with an introduction by David Tr

Footba Mania

The players and the fans the mass psychology of foot

close connection with moral attitudes. Pop encourages the notion of the 'quick fix' to every problem, emotional, political, and cultural."

The breakdown of high and low culture divisions is perhaps the most frequently cited, and controversial, dimension of postmodern debates in cultural politics. The selling of 'Italia '90' to the British public through Pavarotti's **Nessun Dorma** (an album track re-released as a single to tie in with the televising of the World Cup) – or, more properly, the promotion of opera, and Pavarotti's records in particular, through global football – is an excellent illustration. Nigel Kennedy's obsessive illustration of fandom for Aston Villa and Vivaldi's **Four Seasons,** while simultaneously wielding a Stradivarius, a claret and blue scarf and a savage haircut, is another. Increasingly, for postmodern fans of this family entertainment New Order's **World In Motion** and Adamski's house-influenced single **Killer** became just another set of musical signs to read alongside the dulcet tones of the 'fat man' from Italy.

The relationship between pop and football is such that this is taken further in a constant crossover between the two 'low' cultures. An 1989 **NME** feature, "Goal Discs", explored every conceivable facet of "The Football-Rock Connection" from the love affair between Man City and Rob Gretton (New Order's manager) through The Housemartin's **London O Hull 4** album title to records such as the Republic of Ireland Soccer Squad's **The Boys In Green** and **Albania! Albania!** by the (apocryphal) Albania World Cup Squad. In the past, pop's football base has been represented by the standard, stereotypical media figures such as Elton John (Watford's erstwhile Chairman), Rod Stewart (the press' favourite Scotland fan) and Phil Collins (rumoured to be involved in takeover plans at Spurs in 1991).

The term 'Stadium rock' has been given a further twist by the increasing use of football stadia as venues for outdoor pop concerts, not least Wembley Stadium. Julie Burchill's scathing **NME** review of Everton's 1985 FA Cup Final waxing, **Here We Go,** put well the standard view that there is at best a bland, at worst a pathetic, connection between an implicitly streetwise, modern up-to-the-minute,

'def' music business and a musically deaf football world with cloth ears and cloth caps:

> "'Well Brian. Of course you can't entirely divorce football's recent troubles from the social context of unemployment and subsequent frustration in Thatcher's Britain. But a small number of people are striking terror into the hearts of people who really love the game.' 'The government, clubs and the public should make it absolutely clear that they are no longer prepared to tolerate football players making records. But what can be done? Electric fences around the recording studios, water cannons at Top of the Pops, interviews with Paula Yates? The players themselves should set an example. Take me for instance. I'm opening a boutique, Brian'".

Burchill went beyond this rewrite of a Monty Python script to point precisely to this side of football's face, represented so well by the winning West German national team's Eurovision anthem for the World Cup 1990:

> "Everton's chirpy singalong captures the spirit of British football the way Minder crystallises the banality and brutality of the South London underworld."

This mug shot of football is for public (that is, media) consumption only. Like the Python piss-take, it depends on the perpetuation of the image of professional football players and fans as stupid clones barely capable of spouting clichéd babble. Recent musical ventures have deliberately turned Burchill's type of prejudgments on their head. There is a noticeable respect, not to say adoration, from musicians, producers, DJs, music photographers and journalists who are at pains to point out the debt their own 'art' owes to that of the 'people'.

J Saul Kane of Depth Charge signed his 12" single, **Goal** (Vinyl Solution), with the sentence, "Special thanks to all the footballers who made football an art, and gave me countless hours of pleasure". He further cemented the pop/soccer crossover on the record's sleeve and general product design: Side 1 – Yellow Card, Side 2 – Red Card, main mix – First Half, alternative mixes – Second Half + Extra Time and Sudden Death Penalty Shootout respectively.

Band names like Bocca Juniors (from the **Boy's Own**

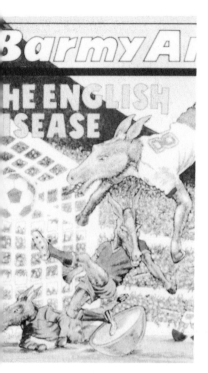

fanzine stable) after Boca Juniors in Argentina, Mexico 70, Lofthouse, Péle and the Bobby Charltons celebrate a famous world football team, a famous event and legendary players. In addition paying homage to the likes of Kenny Dalglish (**Sharp As A Needle**), **Brian Clout**, **Leroy** [Rosenior]**'s Boots**, On-U Sound label owner, Adrian Sherwood, long-time Hammers fan, acknowledged on **The English Disease** album those who "provide vocal support to West Ham United, Liverpool, Manchester City, Blackburn Rovers, Stockport County, Crewe Alexandra, Leyton Orient, Wimbledon and Nottingham Forest", all clubs whose spectators were featured on the samples on the LP. Sherwood also dedicated **The English Disease** (no prizes for spotting the irony in the title, or the 'band' name, The Barmy Army) to "football supporters everywhere" and very definitely not to "those who put profit before safety and comfort, and are disinterested in the voice of those who pay the wages".

The real identification of football supporters (especially those sections most influenced by youth culture) and the players exists in spite of the size of the wage packet and the usually conservative style of most of the game's participants. Fans, in the modern era, have tended to be ahead of the players aesthetically, though footballers are now catching up, opening a cultural pipeline from the terraces to the pitch which has had a greater effect on players' tastes and habits than merely producing new, and sexier, ways of celebrating a goal or simulate fornication with a corner flag. It has, too, given fresh meaning to that favourite football adage 'its all about the fans'.

Until recently the individualist sports like tennis and golf (plus pastimes such as cycling and mountaineering) have been the fashion leaders; even the various casual styles, though born at the football ground, originally reflected a setting of sights on tennis gear rather than football kit. By the time of Italia '90, football (especially Continental and 'away' kits) shirts were *de rigeur* but such fleeting fashion trends have frequently been reintroduced within football's field, copied from other sports and then mixed in with the more familiar expression of popular culture on the terraces – the chant.

While most would agree that Julie Burchill was justified in savaging the generality of football's pop songsters (who could forgive England's 1970 Mexico World Cup horror story, **Back Home**, and all the remixes and outtakes that it spawned, collected for posterity on the Various Artists albums **4-2-4** and **Flair**), the wit and creativity, as well as the potential for violence, of football terrace singing is legendary. Increasingly the popular music industry has incorporated this valuable yet copyright-free commodity.

The use of 'live' terrace chants on Sham '69's **Tell Us The Truth** and Pink Floyd's **Meddle** albums constituted relatively rare musical tributes in the 70s. Even then, though, there was a divide: post-punk, Jimmy Pursey was simply stealing them, taping the audience's football choruses (trying vainly to remind his consumers that the kids are united while neo-fascist skins wrecked his gigs) and, predictably, pre-punk hippies Roger Waters & Co went for a different kind of 'authenticity', using tape of the massed singing, swaying terraces of the 60s and 70s first-hand.

By the early 90s, white rappers First Offence (F-Off – geddit?!), who hail from the same west Salford estate as the Happy Mondays, were able to incorporate the sound of the dated football chant 'You're Gonna Get Your Fucking Heads Kicked In' into their hip-hop dance rhythms with ease, nearly effacing the self-consciously homophobic and reactionary lyrics (for instance, 'I came to watch a soccer match not fairies dancing'). The crossover has, in any case, often been the other way round. Non-football anthems like Manchester band James' **Sit Down**, live at G-Mex (the B-side of their No 1 single), which contained several minutes of fan singalong (complete with whistles and horns) after the band's departure, make many contemporary pop crowds indistinguishable from soccer terrace culture. Predictably, football fans took the song up with Monty Python's **Always Look on the Bright Side of Life** as 90s' singalongs.

Chants themselves come from terrace culture; the songs used, from Gerry and the Pacemakers' 60s hit **You'll Never Walk Alone** onwards, are simply a vehicle for the frequently spontaneous terrace arguments between rival supporters, or between fans and particular players, liked or disliked, on your team or theirs. The tracks so produced soon get remixed, re-released and then deleted, only to reappear in lower division or non-league ex-chart bins.

However, with the rapid technological development in the 80s of samplers and sequencers, and a sonic sensibility (from hip-hop, dub reggae) to the multitude of sounds from urban culture (especially those broadcast on the electronic media, terrace chants, either taped 'live' or recorded from television or radio broadcasts) became ubiquitous. Sports commentaries are, inevitably, a favourite sample. The cut-up voices of the media 'men', backed by a monstrous drum sound and spine-tingling rhythms, resounded on the urban dancefloors in the late 80s and early 90s as much as they did from the radio or small screen in domestic living rooms.

The new 'pop' styles of footballers themselves can also be seen as an extension of terrace culture. The popular music industry's charge to interview anyone who looked like a 'post-punk' footballer in the mid-80s (most music journalists still want to write about football, just as many young football journalists really want to write about music) made most terrace rucks seem tame. Pat Nevin was widely proclaimed as leading a new breed; **NME** christened Nevin the "first" post-punk footballer:

> "The last thing he looks like is an average professional footballer ... out on the park he is one of a rare breed striving to put some joy back into a game slowly choking on its own dour orthodoxy while away from the field he could hardly be further removed from the sick-as-a-moon-over-the-parrot stereotype of the monosyllabic soccer star. An articulate opinionated twenty year old he ... believes passionately in the anti-nuclear movement and is a discerning follower of contemporary rock music ... [who] can wax more coherently and enthusiastically about the current music scene than most of the popsters actually involved in it. His passion is that of the true fan".

Subsequently, Nevin, who transferred to Everton from Chelsea after starting his career at Clyde, has been subjected to media interviews about contemporary 'high' art as well as football and popular music. His deviance from the norm is not just that he has deliberately distanced himself from professional footballers' notoriously insular and 'laddish' culture and embraced a lifestyle closer to the bohemian spectator. Importantly, though his living is earned through work as a footballer, in both spheres – popular music and soccer – his "passion is that of the true fan".

Hillsborough Interlink, a fan magazine produced by and for those affected by Hillsborough, interviewed Nevin in issue eight (the second anniversary issue, April 15 1991) and he stressed his own childhood memories of standing in the "jungle" (kop) at Parkhead as he watched Celtic. He also recalled, poignantly, as a Celtic supporter, the day 66 people died at Rangers' Ibrox ground in 1971. His statement that he had "never felt anything negative about football fans, I've always had a great affair with them" underlines his commitment to giving supporters the right to have a greater say in the game that they finance.

Another **NME** interviewee of the period was Ian Stewart, then a first division player with QPR and a Northern Ireland international but later to taste life in the bargain basement. Stewart, like Nevin, saw the players' relationship to the fans as more significant than the camaraderie of the inward-looking narrowness of the men's locker room. Stewart told **NME** that he thought:

> "the attitude of the players is gradually changing. For three years from 1977 to 1980, the game was getting totally out of hand with all the million pound transfer deals. A lot of players looked down on the fans, but I think that's all over. Football has come down to earth and that's one of the reasons crowds are going up. There are three million unemployed, so footballers cannot afford to think of themselves as anything special".

Setting up his own jokey, satirical fan club was entirely in keeping with Stewart's irreverent attitude to other, more traditional footballers and managers (his greatest claim to fame remains the fact that he was once sacked for "farting" in the assistant boss's car!) and to the supporters who pay a substantial part of his wages came from his background, getting

ALL DONATIONS FOR THIS CARTOON WILL GO TO THE HILLSBOROUGH APPEAL FUND
– THANK YOU G.C.

teenage kicks out of Ulster punk.

Another player interviewed by **NME**, Charlie Nicholas (Brian McClair and John Fashanu were also prominently featured in the 80s), was a much more conventional soccer stylist rather than a radical representative of a 'new breed'. Nicholas, recently arrived at Arsenal when the interview took place, was always a more upwardly mobile star though, like Nevin and Stewart, he was one of a long line of ball-playing Celts who have infiltrated the English league clubs for over a century. At Celtic (where the wayward wanderer returned after a spell at Aberdeen) in the early 80s Nicholas claimed to have built up:

> "a unique rapport with the supporters. Although he was out on the field and they were in the crowd, the fans knew that he was really just one of them".

Such fragile identity, of course, can quickly dissolve as Nicholas himself found during his comparatively unfulfilled career. One of the defining characteristics of the modern era was supposed to have been the end of such 'traditional' football loyalties, based as they were before the 60s on social class and locality. To some extent there was always an element of nonsense in the belief that the past harboured a special relationship between the deferential (mostly) white, working class, male footballer and the peaceful white, working class or lower middle class males who flocked in their thousands to the pleasure domes of industrial England for their weekly (even reserve games were often well attended) fix of the people's opiate. Postmodern footballers and fans are helping to destroy the myths of traditional as well as modern football watching.

One of those myths is the link between football and the construction of masculinity, of maleness. The new (football) man, to the extent that such a figure exists, follows hard on the heels of the New Man in advertising parlance, pop videos and fashion spreads of the 80s (and his successor in the 90s – New Lad). Glossy magazines like **Arena** (male readership offshoot of **The Face**) and **For Him** (with cover stars like John Barnes) have dedicated themselves to the discovery, promotion and marketing of this elusive being.

Another glossy, **GQ** (that's **Gentlemen's Quarterly**) was, by the early 90s, expressing more self-doubt despite its strenuous efforts to create such an object (as rivals from overseas like **Esquire** plumbed more traditional depths of masculinity in the search for sales). In 1991 it ran a feature, "Are You Man Enough?", based on its own questionnaire research into 1,000 men of the 90s (do you dress to please yourself? do you dress to please others? would you cry in front of ...?) and concluded:

> "for all the tumult British men have endured in the past decade our recent GQ & A survey shows them remarkably little changed. What you ask, ever happened to the New Man? And who, we say, ever thought there was one?... British men go into the Nineties bereft of a political mother figure, Margaret Hilda Thatcher having been deposed in a Whitehall coup which once again proved that boys will be boys. In politics so in life. The world may have changed dramatically in the Thatcher decade, but in a survey we carried out during the month of her despatch we discovered much the same profile for successful British men in 1990 as one might have expected in 1980 (or, in all probability, in the year 2000)".

Whether the same skewed comment can be made for the new football fan and the contemporary culture of fandom, or indeed whether it is appropriate to bemoan the absence of a New Football Man, the tracks of Gazza's tears notwithstanding, to replace Arthur Hopcraft's description of yesteryear is debatable. Some commentators and critics say that the game, and consumer culture, is being re-masculinised following the feminist criticisms of the 70s and 80s. **Gay Times** in 1990 claimed the biggest special interest gay group in the country was the Gay Football Supporters Network and in the same year GFSN in Manchester had produced a gay and lesbian football fanzine, **The Football Pink**, which symbolised something of a retort to the tabloids' exploitation of Justin Fashanu's 'coming out'.

Judge for yourselves the significance of contemporary changes in the following history of football's post-war relationship to youth culture and popular music!

THere we went

kenneth wolstenholme black & white version

Ten years is a long time in football; about as long as a week in politics. But a diary of the 1974-75 season looked remarkably similar to one written in the mid-80s though, as this book testifies, in the few years after Heysel, significant changes occurred in fan culture and spectatorship generally. There were pitch invasions, crowd trouble abroad, player 'indiscipline', government concern with hooliganism and the apparent decline of the national game - its image, number of paying spectators, performance of the England team and so on.

A hundred years ago, too, there were magazine articles criticising professionals for their supposed greed, laziness and bad example. Even so a powerful, seductive image of the 'past' as a Golden Age recurs in the culture of English football, as in other aspects of English life. Nostalgia for a particular moment in the game's history is ever present, even if the specific period in question is permanently debated, though it can be generally summed up as a time when there was money in the boots (illegally) rather than from the boots (in sponsorship contracts).

Was English football better in the 20s, 30s or 50s, or even in Edwardian times? Has there really been an improvement in the late 80s and early 90s? If there has, how does it compare with earlier shifts in other decades?

This nostalgic mode compares with the mood of a (then) futuristic novel about football written by Terry Venables ('El Tel' of tabloid legend) with collaborator Gordon Williams. **They Used To Play On Grass** (Mayflower 1973) looked backwards to a (mythical) paradise of skill and style in the early 60s, or maybe even earlier, before Venables burst onto the scene as a player with Peter Bonetti, Jimmy Greaves and the rest of Ted Drake's Ducklings in the late 50s.

Venables and Williams made what were to be remarkably prophetic predictions in the midst of their pulp fiction: Venables himself was later to play for and manage QPR, the first English team to introduce us to the pleasures of the plastic – a journey into the unknown that Luton Town, Preston North End and Oldham Athletic were also to take before Football League regulations reversed the trend to keep off the

OPPOSITE
Man City fans, Maine Road
April 91.

grass. Such prophecies were mixed in with a longing desire for the less grey soccer styles of the past which compared favourably (at least in the authors' eyes) when the book was written in 1971. A character in the book fondly remembers the "glory days" when they used to play on grass:

> "and there on the pitch he began to see players from his past, still doing the things that gave the game its magic ... he saw the salmon leap of Dennis Law, the Viking Scot ... he saw Jimmy Greaves, the little man, gliding past slicing boots and scything legs on a deadly run to goal, protected by invisible rays ... he saw the silky poetry of Alec Young, the man they called the Golden Vision ... he saw the flowing hair of George Best, the little boy genius who had it all ... he saw Bobby Charlton, pride of England ..."

Nearly 20 years later less fictional characters than this sentimental fan were indulging in the same vain search for a lost, fantasy (football) world. When, for instance, Charlton Athletic moved from their historic Valley ground in the 1985-86 season to cross over to Crystal Palace's stadium, Selhurst Park, for what promised to be the first of many long-term ground-sharing schemes, the tears flowed and anger raged. Old memories were stirred; as John Jackson of **The Mirror** told it:

> "I still remember cramming myself onto that towering terrace for a match against Arsenal in 1956 when the gates were shut after 70,000 people had clicked through the turnstiles ... Seventy year-old Sailor Brown joined many old players introduced to the crowd on Saturday. He said: 'I looked up at the huge terrace and I heard the roar of 70,000 throats".

But with those glory, glory days fading fast from Jackson's memory rewind he noted that "today's football climate with its hooliganism and anti-social behaviour would not allow such a crowd." The death of the Valley, moreover, signified the state of the nation's football:

> "British soccer is going bust. The decision by Charlton Athletic and Crystal Palace to share one ground seven miles away at Selhurst Park may well be prophetic ... As Ted Croker, once a Charlton player, now secretary of the Football Association, said 'this could be the beginning of a new era. If this

sort of move can defray the costs for a club, then it must be good. Loyalty and traditions die hard. I am just sad that the guinea pig is my old club'... Television personality Jimmy Hill, a Charlton director, faced mobs of angry supporters on Saturday. They wore black ties, laid wreaths on the centre spot and held a sit-in on the pitch at half-time. And when the final whistle had blown, they took away lumps of turf for keepsakes. Hill said 'This sort of decision is never easy, but lack of money makes it inevitable'... Emotion at times washed away the talk of the hard realities of soccer life".

Charlton fans expressing roughly the same sentiments, though not in such sentimental fashion, organised themselves over the next few years so that these "hard realities of soccer life" were severely challenged while Jimmy Hill, as Chairman, took Fulham to the end of its love affair with Craven Cottage. The **Voice of the Valley** football fanzine, along with other Charlton Athletic fans' 'zines, campaigned strongly for a return of the football club to its original premises. In January 1990, when Greenwich Council turned down the club's planning application to redevelop the derelict Valley ground in line with Lord Justice Taylor's all-seater recommendations, a new political party, the Valley Party, was created to contest virtually every local seat in that year's council elections. By March 1991 pressure group tactics had at long last paid off and the return to the old stadium, with a much reduced capacity, was ensured.

Nostalgia, however, is a pervasive theme in professional football and its effect can be dangerously debilitating for 'traditionalists' taking on the 'modernisers', and vice versa. There is a tendency to paint a romantic picture of soccer's history bordering on the unbelievable, if not the outright fantastic. It rapidly becomes contrasted with a 'realism' which club boardrooms and League and Association officials are said to be applying in order that professional football in its 'mother country' might hobble towards 2000 on crutches.

Soccer styles, on and off the pitch, are also themselves prisoners of this Britannia 'rool'. But were players and football grounds better in the 50s? Was football in England more entertaining when players were poorer and more deferential? Were they more patriotic? What did centre partings, Brylcreem (a revival story in the 80s), dubbin and leather 'casies' have to do with style?

When skiffle hero Lonnie Donegan (the man who was to go on to record **World Cup Willie/Where in This World Are We Going?** in 1966) hit the charts in 1957 with **Gambling Man/Putting On The Style**, industrial relations in the domestic football industry were about to enter a critical phase. The maximum wage was soon to be abolished, another national institution biting the dust along with the famous England manager, Walter Winterbottom, and, eventually, its in-house media voice, Kenneth Wolstenholme.

Wolstenholme: his 1966 World Cup commentary remains with us in disembodied moments sampled for vinyl – "Some people are on the pitch/they think it's all over/it is now!" (also an album title for The Dentists); his image remains as captain in the bizarre 1966 BBC commentators team picture (Coleman, Bough etc) which adorns the I, Ludicrous EP, **Quite Extraordinary**. A new era, 'modern' football, was on the immediate horizon.

Football in the 50s, even if that description cut into the next decade to include the 'traditional' footballers of Tottenham Hotspur's 1961 League and Cup winners, was significant for its position as just about within the recall of the popular memory of many of today's older fans and as the last time soccer players were popularly regarded as having a legitimate grievance over wages and conditions. Spurs' team, built in the 50s on the maximum wage system, was the last of the great British club sides to be viewed with almost untainted nostalgia. Later teams' success was always tinged with media suspicion of players (in reality only a few) who were 'greedy', or made 'outrageous' wage – or salary, as they had now become – claims. **Guardian** sports journalist, David Lacey, reviewing manager Bill Nicholson's autobiography **Glory, Glory – My Life With Spurs** recalled the context of the League and Cup team's triumph:

" Then, as now, football was in decline. The Munich air crash of 1958 had destroyed Manchester United, who represented the domestic game's brightest future, and Wolverhampton Wanderers, while still successful were no longer the force they had been for most of the 50s ... The quality of Tottenham's play, the individual skills of Blanchflower, White, Mackay, Smith and Jones, which were harnessed to the team effort, without ever being stifled by it, gave those fortunate enough to witness their matches the feeling that English League football was being reborn. Now we know that Spurs' Double was really marking the end of an era".

The argument ran that the 1961 abolition of the maximum (and, significantly, eventually the minimum) wage and the 1963 George Eastham High Court case were to make it impossible for teams ever again to be constructed on this model. Generous salaries, freedom of contract and the

"fear of failure and financial loss which soon began to be reflected in negative attitudes on the field after the Double season, have made it extremely difficult to be entertaining and successful."

This is not all idle sentiment by any means; there is a kernel of rationality here among Lacey's look-back-in-anger at today's football flaws.

Clearly the 'trad' era did in some senses receive its final curtain call with the onset of the mid-60s which ushered in a 'mod' phase more generally characterised by negativity. In 1971 Hunter Davies described how Nicholson, still at White Hart Lane as manager, strove for "lightness and brightness, for excitement and skills and, above all, for entertainment. In an era of defence, he has dreamt only of attack". But there is a danger in overemphasising the break from traditional to modern. Those commentators and spectators who watched the 50s' styles, developing out of post-war austerity, join Nicholson himself in a romantic dreamworld by swallowing wholesale the belief that standardised wages in themselves, prior to the 60s, gave teams their essential morale, spirit and 'democracy' which left them distinguishable from the spectating millions only by their skill.

Such mythology has become pernicious in the soccer industry. It has helped clubs fight a rearguard action against the full implications of the abolition of the maximum wage and the introduction of freedom of contract for players in anything but the most limited form. It has also given sustenance to those who hold

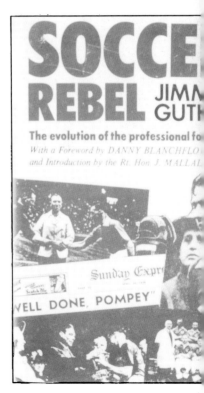

the view, expressed by former Football League secretary, Alan Hardaker, in his autobiography, **Hardaker of the League.** This was, effectively, that the ending of the maximum wage had the status of something like a crime against humanity and should never be accepted as a *fait accompli.* Failure to adapt satisfactorily to the changes implied by the events of the early 60s, and the consequent replay of imaginary and irrelevant battles, has been a major reason for the continued economic malaise of the football industry since the 60s.

Similar myth-making has underscored the performance of the English national team. The modern era virtually opened with the winning of the 1966 World Cup, its last true triumph on the world stage … notwithstanding the quarter-final disappointments of Mexico in 1970 and 1986 and an unexpected trip to the semi-finals in the Italia '90 tournament.

In 1981, some months prior to the Falklands War, in what was seen widely in the mass media as an ignominious away defeat by a 'small' country (Norway in a World Cup qualifier) a Scandinavian commentator's shrieks of euphoria were constantly repeated for television viewers, especially his roll call of English national heroes from the imperial and colonial past, including Lord Nelson and Winston Churchill. The quip "Are you listening, Maggie Thatcher, Maggie Thatcher your boys took a hell of a beating" almost scanned like a terrace chant.

The Daily Mail sports journalist, Jeff Powell, blamed increased payments to players for international appearances, on top of 'high' club wages, as the reason for this apparently spectacular national sporting failure. In one sense this was just another familiar World Cup slip-up against, in tourist and sporting mythology, a nothing nation fit only for fjords and rally driving, everyday fodder for a press still dozily dreaming of the Boy's Own days of Empire. Powell, however, along with many of his journalistic colleagues, went to town on the symbolic consequences of decline, national and sporting.

Instead of contemplating the fact that the performance of England's Boys of '66 may itself have been consistently overvalued and that previously 'soft touch' nations were rapidly catching up those fortunate

enough to be considered by FIFA as worthy of World Cup seeding (remember Algeria and Cameroon in 1982, Morocco in 1986, Egypt and Cameroon again in 1990?), **The Mail** let loose a scathing attack on 'greedy, unpatriotic, overpaid and over there' international stars. Jeff Powell argued that such players should play for England for nothing and be pleased about it. In fact, lessons in the evils of sporting mammon, when playing for the old country, were probably less relevant here than asking which internationals had been on the bevvy the night before the match because they believed everything they had read in the same papers about their part-time opponents and reckoned they could risk it.

Nevertheless, the magnetism of pre-'modern' days was once more irresistible. To support its line and wallow in the nostalgia, **The Mail** chose to wheel out one Bobby Charlton, a star name with clean credentials and renowned enough in English (sporting) history to be included in the Norwegian commentator's list. Charlton's role in the days of 1966 is legendary, but essentially he played as a born-again midfielder who gave Alf Ramsey's wingless wonders a touch of world-class.

In response to the Norwegian defeat, Charlton recalled an earlier international, and domestic, era following the Second World War and prior to the abolition of the maximum wage. What characterised this period for Charlton, who came into the profession in the tail end of these years, was the lack of social distance between players and supporters. In Charlton's mind the similar social milieu inhabited by players and fans was connected inextricably to performance.

In an article, "England, My England", attributed to Charlton and **Mail** man John Roberts, the old international argued that "the public have lost sympathy with footballers … Just after the war players seemed to belong to the society in which they played". As Jeff Powell had already said on the same sports pages "Blame The Money!" – but just as the nation's 'ignominious' defeats in the 50s, first by the USA and twice, in some style, by the Hungarians, seemed to have escaped the old player's memory, so the exact connections between players, clubs, administrators and fans became somewhat clouded in

the mists of time.

If anything captured the life and times of the professional footballer in 50s England it was that curious combination of deference with respectability. Stanley Matthews, the eternal 'Mr Football', put it best in his early autobiography, **Feet First Again** (still available from car boot sales, Corgi Special 1955):

> "I am grateful also to the Football Association and appreciated the address and the certificates presented to me when I broke the international appearances record. Football has been kind to me. But most important of it all it has provided me with thousands of true friends. They are on the terraces each week".

Matthews' own pristine reputation was to be somewhat tarnished by football scandal in later years but this view from the 50s reeked of soccer servility: a humble worker who knew his place and was grateful for any extra crumbs that fell off the top table. No one who saw Matthews in the flesh could doubt his unbelievable dribbling skill – though he didn't exactly tackle, score goals or head the ball very often! But it was the ideal picture of the traditional footballer which he represented so well that makes his deference so significant.

It is precisely that style of club 'servant' that many of the reform proposals from the game's governing bodies have been designed to resurrect ever since. Skilful and dutiful: a winning combination! Jimmy Armfield, a colleague of Matthews' at Blackpool in the 50s and the players' representative there, has gone so far as to suggest that the employers could have got away with preserving the maximum wage system in its entirety in the early 60s, if only they had been prepared to increase the £20 winter maximum.

Many of the crop of various journalistic and sociological studies of football are tarred by this same romantic brush, though they are just as often coloured by strongly expressed passion for players' rights. Their nostalgia for the past – and particularly the 50s – stems, essentially, from seeing, in players like Matthews, figures with impeccable manual working class credentials, before their brethren became seduced by the consumerism of the 60s, 70s

and 80s. The problem is that things were never that clear-cut: Matthews' father may have been a boxer but he also owned his own barber's shop. It was not always possible to describe professional footballers as if they had just come off the night shift underground. Even the most observant of football's critics tend to romanticise the class origins of soccer players. David Triesman, in his introduction to **Football Mania**, recalls from the 50s (where else?) the "Lion of Vienna" ... otherwise known as Nat Lofthouse:

> "a player who ... had been a Bevin boy in the last war, a coal pit face worker conscripted for work in the mines rather than military service. Lofthouse, like so many other footballers came off the terraces, the son of a coal man, and he went into first-class football on a £1-10s-0d weekly wage".

The strains of the music to the Hovis advert can almost be heard in the background ... used, with heavy irony, in recent years by Southern fans to taunt visiting spectators from the North.

Another of soccer's oral history chroniclers, Dave Robins, passsed on the reminiscences of a post-war Man City fan who recalls when Maine Road had:

> "a very mixed crowd. There was a lot of old blokes, and women, even some elderly women. You all stood together. You knew everybody. You never saw 'em between games. But we always stood in roughly the same place and we knew the forty or fifty people around us 'cos they were always there. The worst hazard of standing in that crowd was someone pissing down the back of your leg. But now its getting a bottle on your head and that's a different thing altogether. It takes the fun out of it".

In this version of all our yesterdays being 'pissed wet through' meant exactly what it said ... ah! the good old bad old days. What is really at issue is not that such descriptions provided an idealised picture of particular aspects of professional football in the 50s but that they are taken as representing general trends, in sport and society, which are then compared (favourably or unfavourably, depending on the context) with the present.

These myths of romanticised traditional football persisted well into the modern era ... until, eventually, enough clubs began to modernise amenities, like seats, bars and toilet facilities, to well and truly

OPPOSITE
Munich 58 graffiti
near Oldham, May 91.

The White Hart Lane Mystery

erase the image of 20,000 Koppites clutching their rolled-up match programmes in case they got caught short before half-time.

However, until the Taylor Report none of this 'modernising' of football meant that fans could not stand together in the same place on the terraces year after year enjoying the gentle sarcasm of the crowd, the pathetic failure of their team to score or simply the brilliance of the visiting team's goalkeeper. The danger in panaceas such as all-seater stadia is that, contrary to the learned judge's manifest intentions, they will be presented as solutions to the problem of violence rather than stadium safety and decay, as ways of rescuing the traditional game from the modern game's hooliganism … while every terrace in sight is bulldozed so that the clubs can put more 'bums on seats' and more money in the bank.

More important than all this, though, is the conflation, in popular memory, of the 50s with a moment in the game when the uncoached, natural football ability of the British working man made virtually its last stand. That is, before it irrevocably surrendered to the modern era with its master coaches (Allison, Greenwood, Revie, Howe, Robson, Kendall, Taylor) ready and waiting to confuse them.

The notion that only the modern era had witnessed the appliance of soccer science (tactics, drawing boards, team dossiers and all the rest) is, of course, an historical nonsense but the memory of the day an era, and a team, died lingers on.

The Munich air disaster, which called an abrupt end to the Busby Babes, decimated a side containing the likes of Duncan Edwards and hangs, even today, like a pall over Old Trafford. The death of many of the domestic game's brightest hopes (and the survival of Bobby Charlton and Busby himself) symbolised both the shattering of traditional football style and the rebirth, in a much more hostile decade, of its most significant component: the umbilical cord between soccer fans and attacking, exciting, skilful styles of play.

Eclipsing the memory of even the great Man United team of the late 40s, the 1958 air crash almost single-handedly established the club's awesome spectator pulling-power which has drawn such

enormous international support for the last 30 years. Simultaneously it lit the already smouldering fuse of hyper-local and regional rivalries which underwrote the hooligan battles of the 70s and 80s and culminated in the scrawled graffiti of the 90s, recalling the more contemporary disaster of Hillsborough and the global packaging of the Manchester pop music scene, which reads 'Madchester vs Merseydied'.

'We only hate Man United ...' has echoed the reaction of thousands of spectators when this particular Red Army has come to, or crossed town, in modern times. The fact that the club's average home gates have been consistently twice as high as most of even their First Division competitors is still linked, however tenuously, to the Munich disaster. This for a club whose last League Championship win was in 1967.

Fans in every port, coaches from all over the country in the car park at every home match, Man United are a national rather than a local team. Their style of organisation since the Munich days has been ever more businesslike, complete, as documented by Michael Crick and David Smith, with club scandal under the chairmanship of Louis Edwards and the ill-fated attempt of his son, Martin Edwards (as salaried Chief Executive), to sell the major shareholding to unknown businessman and former footballer, Michael Knighton.

A multinational giant corporation (Premier League supporters, along with the rest of the 'Big Five') in a footballing nation of small shopkeepers, Man United's playing styles have perhaps been more closely scrutinised than any other club. A commitment to positive, attacking football with flair, in an era when not losing (that is, "getting a result"), has always been more important to the manager's peace of mind on Saturday night or Sunday morning.

Over the years mass public sympathy for the tragic loss of virtually a whole team in unnatural circumstances was translated to associate the team and individual playing styles with 'going forward' (it is always Man United's attacking players that are revived in popular memory: Best, Charlton, Law rather than Sadler, Brennan, Dunne) to such an extent that Dave Sexton's ultra-modernist approach cost him the manager's chair at Old Trafford despite reasonable League positions.

It is still remarkable how the somewhat ghostly presence of the 'lost' team haunts succeeding sides. Even the 60s' model was always fettered by Sir Matt Busby's much-proclaimed need to win the European Cup (an accomplishment believed close at hand when the 50s version crashed) in a barely sublimated desire to avenge deep anger, personal grief and public loss.

The final closure of the story, the 1968 European Cup Final victory at Wembley over Benfica (or Nobby Stiles' over Eusebio – immortalised in Too Much Texas' song **Heart of Jesus**) was achieved at the eventual future cost of killing another team, albeit less painfully, but just as surely, as its most prominent individualist, George Best, slid into despair. As Best, who scored a brilliant goal, recalled in his third, and most factual, autobiography **Where Do I Go From Here?** (the one before **The Good, The Bad and The Bubbly**) :

> "The adrenalin slowed and I could feel myself no longer part of the laughter and the tears. I was there but I didn't belong. All around me were men and women for whom this was the greatest night of their lives; the climax of all the years of planning, tragedy, disappointment and determination. It should have been that for me. Instead, although I was not to know it at the time, it was the beginning of the end".

Busby's mission accomplished, Best slipped down the slope to alcoholism as he witnessed the break-up of the team which came on as substitute after 1958 to become the first English club to win the premier European prize. In a way this was 'traditional' football's final fling.

Man City fans' taunts for their 'Manc' rivals in the mid-80s such as 'There's only one United – a biscuit' and (at Maine Road Derbies) 'You only came in a taxi' might have found their way onto the pages of the 70s magazine **Foul**.

Foul, the product of a group of Cambridge University students, was football's only 'alternative' paper of the period and seemed destined for longevity. It may have survived longer if its later writers, like Stan Hey and Andrew Nickolds, had not gone on to pastures new in television sitcom/drama and sports journalism (Hey wrote Channel 4's **The Manageress** and became chief sports editor at the short-lived **Sunday Correspondent**). As fanzine fan, Pat Nevin, argued in 1991:

> "[fanzines] keep football clubs on their toes and they keep the game on its toes. It started with things like 'When Saturday Comes' but a long time ago, in the '70s, the original one was a magazine called 'Foul' ... If 'Foul' had been allowed to develop, then the fans would have had their say. Its just sad that after all the troubles we've had, fanzines are only developing and have a say now".

In the early-mid 70s **Foul** was essentially football's **Private Eye**, serving as a protest against the years of boring, defensive, dull and dirty team styles which mushroomed in the late 60s and early 70s. It stood as a lone monument, a radical attempt to intervene, however jokily, in the mass media and politics of professional soccer in Britain. It symbolised a moment in the history of the game, especially via the clipped title of the magazine, which witnessed a deliberate tactical stifling of skill and flair. Styles, and the game, had moved on by the time a collection of **Foul** golden oldies was published in 1976, but it is significant that the late 80s football fanzine movement chose to recognise **Foul's** achievement with a special collection over a decade later, edited by Mike Ticher who, with Andy Lyons, was **When Saturday Comes'** first editor. **Foul** certainly protested about the dirty tricks abounding in English professional soccer (and, especially, the mass media) at the beginning of the 70s – previously put down in the press to 'overseas' influences – but it wasn't simply the roughness and cynicism of playing styles that were seeping into the nation's premier spectator sport which was at stake. No one was actually being killed and way back to the 1880s there had already been plenty of ruthless 'cloggers' in football's professional history who had, literally, threatened fellow players' life and limb – much as Italia '90 hero Schillaci had done in a later League game. It was, rather, the calculated collaboration of so many of the game's participants (no single group escaped blame) in its (alleged) stylistic decline which motivated the lethal mix of biting satire and investigative journalism that graced

see pages 3 & 10

41

Foul's pages between 1972 and 1976.

However, the ethos of the magazine was hamstrung by a nostalgia for a bygone era. To some extent this was inevitable; consider how contemporary football fanzines celebrate the 70s' maverick entertainers such as Peter Osgood, Alan Hudson, Tony Currie, Frank Worthington, Duncan MacKenzie and Stan Bowles. Though geared to an aesthetic defence of the 60s' playing stylists (Best and co), Foul harked back to that mythical Golden Age of the 50s as if the long march of football's creative talent ended, or went into reverse, when Jimmy Guthrie, chair of the Players' Union, was unceremoniously succeeded by sweet-talking, upwardly-mobile guy, Jimmy Hill.

In October 1976 Foul carried an interview with Guthrie, a former Portsmouth player whose self-styled militancy has become something of a yardstick used to beat any of the so-called moderates who either preceded or followed his own term of office at the union in the 40s and 50s. The occasion was the publication of his autobiography, Soccer Rebel, and the article (by Foul original Alan Stewart) concluded that:

> "the book serves to remind the present smug and apathetic leadership of the PFA that the Union did once have a more radical chairman, and that the ideal of winning the war in order to disband the army is not one to be despised".

Foul frequently did lash the PFA of the early 70s with the then chair, former Wolves player Derek Dougan, being a particular target. The main charges were weakness (PFA, the magazine suggested, really stood for Pretty Feeble Altogether) and using the official positions of the organisation for self-aggrandisement – going into television, football management or business. Guthrie certainly claimed that his sole aim was to make the union's function redundant, in his words "to make footballers free", and did energetically court the labour and trade union movement, an activism undertaken by no other union footballer since Charlie Roberts much earlier in the century.

But the fact is that he frequently lost the confidence of the Players' Union management committee and it was Hill who successfully negotiated the conditions of a new era after Guthrie's acrimonious departure at a time when the membership was more focussed on an increase to, rather than the abolition of, the maximum wage.

It is perhaps fitting that the foreword to Guthrie's reminiscences was penned by the captain of Spurs' double side, Danny Blanchflower. Just as Blanchflower is remembered as the skilled leader of the last great football club team of 'working class heroes', Tom Finney and Stanley Matthews revered as the last of the dignified, deferential master craftsmen of the 'art', so Guthrie is resurrected in the modern era as the last great politically conscious 'traditional' union footballer.

After Guthrie, so the story goes, the Union became an 'Association' and was the willing midwife to the 'middle class' or 'bourgeois' footballer who wanted none of Guthrie's principles of collective solidarity with 'the people' who paid to watch the game. In this popular mythology even the game's status as an 'art' was eventually questioned by Steve Coppell, one of Guthrie's successors at the PFA (where he formed an important young, progressive axis with Gordon Taylor), who, after several years of management at Crystal Palace, confessed to The Times in May 1990 before his team's surprise appearance in the FA Cup Final:

> "You have to decide if football is an art form or a science. At first I believed it was an art form, now I recognise it's a science. The game is changing. You can get by with systems rather than players".

Foul's much-needed irreverence towards the football world – which contemporary football fanzines have multiplied many-fold to try to make sure they won't get Fouled again – hid a serious, investigative side to the magazine. It acted as a forum and training ground for some of the best football writers to emerge in the 70s and 80s. Eamon Dunphy, for instance, whose diary of (part of) a soccer season as a Millwall player still stands as a far more accurate 'day-in-the-life-of-a-professional-footballer' than all the glossy biopics put together, was given space to sharpen his pen ... perhaps in preparation for his furious journalistic battle over the Republic of Ireland's playing style with Jack Charlton, the only 'Boy of

OPPOSITE
Goodison Park
May 91.

'66' to graduate to international team management. In one particularly vitriolic onslaught on the PFA, published by **Foul** under the heading "Part of the Union Or The Mill Owner's Charter" Dunphy argued that:

> "The image of the Professional Footballer as a glamorous show-business type surrounded by pretty girls and flash cars is firmly implanted in most people's minds. I know him more accurately as the deeply insecure family man or the tearful failed Apprentice. Getting that image across is what the Professional Footballers Association, the players union, should be all about. And while it is often said that Trade Union movement in Britain is too powerful, the equation between Union and power in football contains an element of black comedy. The PFA is a small organisation ... comprising largely apathetic members. We have, in fact, practically no say in the game's decision-making process, there is no consultation process, and very little consideration of the players' point of view. It is a situation no normal Trade Union or professional body would tolerate for a moment. Consequently, our conditions of employment are such that a reincarnated 19th century mill owner would be gratified to see that restrictive practices so dear to his heart are alive and well in football. Men can still be bought and sold in the market place, apprentices [sic] are callously dismissed on completion of their apprenticeship, and the possibility of retirement through injury without compensation, looms over every game - an additional tension in an already high-risk profession. The existence of such conditions could be regarded as a massive indictment of the PFA. However, this would be an oversimplification".

A platform was also provided for journalists who were later to achieve stature in writing critically and inventively about sport, and especially soccer. For example, Peter Ball (who collaborated with Dunphy) and Chris Lightbown were granted the opportunity to develop their insights into 70s soccer culture, particularly press reporting of football.

But the death-throes of modern football were still some years away when **Foul** was proudly billing itself as "Football's Alternative Paper", though it certainly constituted the writing-on-the-wall ... the warning of what was to come. It said what (mainly) young, white, male, middle class fans were saying out loud on the terraces every week during much of the 70s;

it merely said it in a **Private Eye** format which ridiculed everyone and anything in its wake. It was a meeting place, too, for those who argued for various versions of 'real' football watching.

Ten years after **Foul**, John Peel, popular music DJ who has championed Liverpool Football Club and indie music alike for 30 years, ran his 'Campaign For Real Football' on national radio. In **City Limits** in 1983 Peel contended that:

> "football does not need brightening up, at least not in the way Jimmy (Hill) and his chums advocate ... No, we must unite, brothers and sisters against those who would wreck football. 'And who are those wreckers?', I hear you cry. I name the football authorities and a disturbing number of those who report and comment on the game ... When experts discuss the critical lack of interest in football ... they overlook – or dare not suggest – that those who run the clubs ... are woefully out of touch. In their anxiety to milk revenue from their game before it collapses completely they make decisions which alienate the most dedicated of fans."

In the early 70s similar arguments were raging. One outraged **Foul** correspondent of the period complained:

> "What the hell is all this we keep hearing about 'Family Football'. 'More Seated Accommodation' and 'Restrict Movement on the Terraces'? Is this the fate for football in the future? The Game seems to be turning its back on the real supporters in favour of the Season Ticket family and their admittedly greater money. But will they, Mum Dad, Auntie Doris and the kids, go to a game in the middle of winter at the other end of the country when there is a rail strike on? Will they Hell? Football is not about covered stadiums, padded seats, ice cream, and women and kids. It's about hitching, getting pissed, shouting, standing, pushing, pissing on your boots or the guy in front's legs, singing, chanting, surging and swaying, scarves and if you feel like it AGGRO!
>
> The more we try and make the middle class frightened of coming to games, the more they are excluding us, fencing us in and restricting our movement on the terraces. So bad is this getting that they have put up barriers on the Kop to stop that famous surge. What next? A ban on singing? No scarves allowed? No standing room? It's coming unless we do something about it".

This singularly prophetic, not to mention sexist, vision from the 70s of the shape of things to come for the football industry is an instance of what Ian Taylor had already called soccer's subcultural resistance to the "embourgeoisement" of the game. Suggestions for doing 'something about' this transformation of what was perceived as a 'working class' game into a middle class leisure business abounded in the pages of **Foul**.

In one even more anarchistic letter, a correspondent laid out his vision of the possibilities of "fighting back rather than each other" when "we should be uniting in hundreds of thousands as defiant, resentful kids" not "blindly and fearfully lashing out at anything that wears the wrong colour scarf". He also sketched in what he thought the young "pissed on" males of English soccer should be uniting against:

> "Apparently well-meaning chaps like Gordon Jago and Jimmy Hill will destroy football if allowed any sort of administrative power. Their Utopia is a spotless concrete bowl lined with thousands of little blue plastic seats, lots of clean toilets, a restaurant, a sports complex, piped muzak and 22 clean-cut, goal-hungry young zombies playing the game in a spirit of friendship and sportsmanship on a plasti-grass pitch. They want matches which end in 7-7 draws, watched by packed crowds of middle class parents who have each brought their 2.4 children who cheer enthusiastically every goal, applaud every exhibition of skill from the opposition and who go home afterwards in their family saloons, all agreeing that they have been thoroughly entertained. Bollocks to their visions! It is on those cold forbidding terraces that you find the central nervous system of football from which the adrenalin rises and the lifeblood flows".

During the 70s, and certainly as the 80s wore on, modernisation of the football industry, however uneven, took these sort of backward looks (essentially to the days when mothers, wives and girlfriends sat at home waiting for their young men to come back from the football front) by the scruff of the neck. **Foul**, though a pioneer at first, was in fact not alone in its counter-cultural criticisms of the football industry. The short-lived **Leveller** magazine took up **Foul's** cudgels even as **Foul** was nearing its end, while

an equally ephemeral late-80s publication, **The News on Sunday**, allowed troubadour Attila The Stockbroker to prove that the pen is mightier than the chord with a series of feather-ruffling pieces on soccer culture. **The Leveller**'s pilot issue in February 1976 carried on the earlier interventions in the debates between 'traditionalists' and 'modernisers' by focusing on the archaic, and unique, industrial relations in the football business. Alan Stewart, transferred from **Foul**, journeyed to Scotland, where the Scottish PFA had recently affiliated to the General and Municipal Workers Union (as it was then), to interview Jackie McNamara, Celtic's rare breed – a member of the Communist Party. When asked how far he had succeeded in convincing his team-mates to support the "working class struggle" McNamara wistfully replied:

> "I have tried the odd time, but you just get shut up right away because they're not interested, they're detached from the struggle. I can only talk about Celtic Park. There aren't many who are politically conscious at all. They are in it for the wages and that's all".

Beyond a tinge of Red Clyde nostalgia was a recognition in this self-styled "new radical examiner" that the 'freedom of contract' dispute, then in a bitter phase, was more than just a sell-out by the union, and that rank and file members and the general public set conditions on its operations which could be debilitating. In an article entitled "We Was Robbed", John Allen highlighted Steve Perryman (one of another rare breed, a Labour voting Spurs player) as emphasising the more serious side of the insecurity of the football world of work when he spelt out the soccer player's lot: "I talk about going to work and people laugh, they think you just kick a ball around on a Saturday afternoon".

Allen noted too that, even in 1977:

> "The popular image, heroes of the working class getting rich quick for working $1\frac{1}{2}$ hours a week, and the entrenched attitudes of the game's governing body of employers (club chairpersons who look after the game in their spare time) have resulted in feudal working conditions for professional footballers. Treated as fleshy capital, investments

who only think through their feet, they are unable to change jobs without their current employer demanding cash from their would-be employer. No other worker in Britain suffers such restriction of movement".

To blame the PFA, as football's syndicalist critics did, in these circumstances for acting "more like an advisory service than a trade union, particularly at club level" and for "propping up a system that benefits a footballers' aristocracy at the expense of the rest" is really to have the cake and some more. The ending of the maximum wage and the Eastham court case, such a celebrated cause for sports politics and in popular memory ever since, effectively revolutionised the union's position so that it could never again be regarded as either a blue collar or white collar trade union simply bargaining over wages and conditions. Like it or not, whoever led the organisation, its position was fundamentally transformed from the early 60s onwards; rebels without a clause!

Its role models were other international team sport player associations, and increasingly as time went on it found itself, in effect, bailing out a crisis-ridden industry as the shambling amateurs of the FA and FL ran the good ship Football aground.

Foul and **The Leveller** provided much needed rhetorical backing for professional footballers' renewed 'freedom' campaign in the 70s but the terrain on which the PFA was now fighting proved entirely different from the football feudalism and soccer slavery of the 50s. The age of the global mass media and consumer society was upon us.

Just how necessary the brief period of intervention by football's 70s radical press proved to be was highlighted by the new football media of the 80s. Another short-lived publication, **Football Kick**!, provided a case in point.

This was veritably the yuppies' revenge on **Foul**; it was glossy, 'adult-oriented' (that is, it featured, prominently, colour pictures of semi-nude female models adorned in football kit) and came complete with sharply right-wing editorials; a real footballing **Penthouse**. This self-proclaimed "Greatest Ever Football Magazine" for "grown-ups" was, by issue

8 in November 1982, already calling for the (Thatcher) government to implement its 'law and order' policies in the field of football (and footballer) hooliganism. It carried ex-Arsenal and Leicester City player (later manager of Millwall) Frank McLintock's trip down memory lane as he recalled, from his Glasgow youth, a certain Judge Carmont who was fond of dishing out 16-year jail sentences at the drop of a razor. In Frank McLintock's view the early 80s football hooligan problem would soon have been over if the methods of the man who "put the skids under the Scottish slashers" were adopted. Who needed **The Sun** when **Football Kick**! was on the bookstalls?

Football's star treatment of players – their favourite colour, car, women – so-beloved of football programme editors has had a certain systematic exploitation in the 70s and 80s if not quite the overkill accorded to, say, the popular music industry. **The Face's** younger and short-lived sibling, **The Hit**, featured star strikers in hi-tech poses while the re-styled versions of long-standing weeklies like **Shoot** and **Match** attempt a 'pop star'.format.

On the other hand, what **Foul** really had going for it was its 'traditional' style and themes flying in the face of incipient modernisation of the game. It read like a Charlie Cooke virtuoso performance; if it had been published later it would have carried 'tricky' Mickey Thomas' wink at the cameras (at one time replayed for millions of viewers each weekend on television credits) after an opponent's supposed foul tackle.

Since **Foul's** demise there remained certain, rather uneven, sources of football journalism outside the national press. For instance, in the 80s and 90s, **Football Monthly** and **World Soccer** have been joined by **Football Today**, **Ninety Minutes** and **Non-League Football** as railway station reading.

But the real trainspotters, as this book shows, have been football fanzines themselves, providing, in a hyperreal television and video age, a sense of critical humour which has been sorely missing in the rest of the print media and an obsessive eye for the minutest of detail. This glaring absence in the printed word – an inability to laugh at the industry which it takes so seriously, yet blatantly lets off the hook when the

chips are really down – has left the field free for 'Saint and Greavsie' to increasingly parody itself as well as ridicule Scottish goalkeepers and Hamilton Academicals till the cows come home; and to practice their own brand of nostalgia for a time when they themselves joined the ranks of the professional footballer – yes, you've guessed it, the 50s!

Disappearing 60s' heroes like Ian St John and Jimmy Greaves – along with the likes of Dennis Law and Terry Venables who lingered on into the 70s – now make curtain calls as football's media men, called on as representing the essential, 'authentic' dimension of professional football before the modern era really took hold. They are seen as throwbacks to the traditional era who were mangled by commercial exploitation and defensive tactics produced by 'modernisation'. In the tragic cases of Greaves and George Best, they were driven into alcoholism and a very early bath just as their careers should have been peaking.

This view of authenticity does not, of course, allow for changes in fitness, style of dress, weight of ball, pattern of play and so forth. Greaves, to his credit, though still maintaining that "years ago there were more thrills and spills" acknowledged in a **City Limits** interview in the mid-80s that:

> "It's totally different. Players are fitter, more versatile – when I played you could tell a full back by size, height and weight – and better pitches and playing gear all go to help. But then you've created stalemate."

Few who witnessed the Italia '90 spectacle could doubt the accuracy of the old campaigner's words but, in truth, it is the dead weight of traditional memory which has almost killed modern football every bit as much as tales of hooliganism and get-rich-quick merchants. Team and individual styles have clearly fluctuated since the late 50s but there is no easy return to 'authentic' football. It is now literally a different ball game from the days which spawned the 70s' critics of the cultural spectacle that is professional football.

OPPOSITE
Police and fans
Boundary Park, May 91.

HEY mister can we Have our Ball Back?

flippin' heck ref, that was a foul surely

Ever since the beginning of modern football the same debates have raged: how much 'live', how many action replays, how much analysis by 'experts'? When Blackpool played Bolton Wanderers on a Saturday night in the early 60s for a television experiment – two great names of the traditional era performing the last rites on a Golden Age, black and white traditionalists waiting for colour TV to signal their decline – the scene was set for the creation of a generation of armchair fans.

Millions of soccer enthusiasts, lectured by Jimmy Hill, Bob Wilson and Elton Welsby, were to have their introduction to football history through television. In the 50s what is now the most important carrier pigeon of soccer nostalgia was just a glint in programmers' schedules. Soon the Good Old Days barely existed outside of videotape or receding and confused memories. An era was deemed to be over when an 'historic' manager, whose football roots stretched back over several decades, was unceremoniously scrapped to make way for modern methods and the 'New Look'.

As Martin Hall wrote in a poetry tribute to soccer in **The Stan Cullis Blues** (Charisma 1971) "the night Stan Cullis got the sack/Wolverhampton wandered round in circles/like a disallowed goal/looking for a friendly linesman". Both football and poetry have manifestly suffered at the hands of television's long rapacious march since the 50s. In a late 80s' collection (though the material spanned two decades) 'beat' poetry football celebration, **Here We Go**, Dave Cunliffe argued:

"Association Football – in its myriad skills, sophistication and athleticism – is poetry magic writ large. Some contemporary poetry culture significantly parallels recent soccer history ... Association Football is an High Energy team game which fuses group identification, loyalty and shared belief ... It is an anarchic paradox. A unification of order and chaos. After the kick-off, all is possible. The maverick mystics of the terraces are akin to Norman Mailer's lumpen fifties hipsters 'equally a candidate for the most reactionary and most radical of movements'. Pyschic outlaws both ... High Energy active poetry and soccer followings have simultaneously and temporally declined, leaving

51

dedicated enthusiastic nucleuses. British poets celebrate soccer. Some have and do play. Others are terrace regulars. Poetry and football Establishments beware. Fanatics are afoot."

Other related media have striven, occasionally, to create an "underground and counter-culture" sense of soccer's "celebral orgasm" (in Cunliffe's phrase), its anarchic fun and, moreover, its place in a more palatable future for cultural industries. In **The Rising Sons of Ranting Verse: Cautionary Tales For Dead Commuters** (Unwin1985) Steven (Seething) Wells and Attila The Stockbroker evoked joyous satires on Albanian football and the soccer predelictions of **Sun** readers.

Film representations of soccer culture have been almost universally laughable (remember **Escape to Victory**?). Notable exceptions are Wim Wenders' **The Goalkeeper's Fear Of The Penalty** and Bill Forsyth's **Gregory's Girl.** The latter examining, in context, the problems and possibilities of girls playing school football, an activity which is described enthusiastically by the teenage male lead as "modern".

Football and literature have largely been strange bedfellows. Despite being a sometime international goalkeeper (for Algeria in the 30s) Albert Camus did not exactly focus on football in his novels and existential philosophy. In more recent times the connection has been seen more often in a kind of 'soccer with a social conscience' mode of writing and broadcasting. For instance, Dan Kavanagh's novel **Putting The Boot In** (Penguin 1987) managed a mix of AIDS, sexuality and soccer while Channel 4's **The Manageress** at least explored the notion of women managers in football.

There has even been an attempt to create a 'fanzine of the air' with Radio 5's **Bob Hatton Rattle**, fronted by Jim Reeve, football linkman of Piccadilly Gold, and involving fanzine writer and journalist, John Duncan.

However, as journalist Andy Spinoza has argued, it is print fanzines which have been the soccer fans' alternative press in the late 80s and 90s. He claims, justifiably, that at "the end of the 1980s when the government was out to hit fans with an ID card scheme, fans reacted with their own press". Guy Lovelady, editor of **Rodney Rodney** (a fanzine and a record label) suggests that:

"the Heysel stadium disaster in 1985 was the turning point. Fanzines were a reaction to the way the media exploited the behaviour of a small minority. They expressed dissatisfaction with the way most fans are treated, both in and out of football grounds".

Before 1985 there were a mere handful of fanzines in this field. It is now possible to list well over 400 sports-related fanzines (mainly football and almost all produced in Britain and Ireland) which have existed at one time or another. In many ways it is the very existence of football fanzines on such a scale and involving such complex diversity which is noteworthy.

There follows a master list of all such fanzines ever produced, though many are now defunct. The titles alone should be enough to convince the reader that something different is going on, but the idea of a list is, in itself, important.

When Saturday Comes and **The Absolute Game** in particular, and most fanzines in general, have developed the habit of listing, in each issue, the names and addresses of all other fanzines and of sales outlets (including record and sports book shops), and producing an update of new fanzines (and old ones going out of business). It has proved to be a successful format for building an alternative local cultural network in an age dominated by hi-tech global media.

The definitive list, current for 1990/91 season ... where there is no address the magazine is probably defunct:

The Abbey Rabbit
220 Abbotswold, Harlow,
Essex CM18 6TP
Cambridge United fans

The Absolute Game
PO Box 303, Southern DO,
Edinburgh EH9 1NE
General Scottish football

Addickted
4 Dacre Place, London, SE13 5DJ
Charlton Athletic fans

Albania FC
12 The Furrows, Harefield,
Middlesex UB9 6AT
General football in Albania

The Almighty Brian
6 Gray's Inn Buildings, Roseberry
Avenue, London EC1R 4PN
Nottingham Forest fans

Alotta Balls
BBC Main Street, Coatbridge ML5 3RB
General Scottish football

Always The Bridesmaid
10/11 Stenhouse Avenue,
Edinburgh EH11 3HY
Hearts fans

Alternative Kilbowie Komment
23 Beech Drive, Clydebank G81 3QD
Clydebank fans

Alternative Mansfield Matters
29 Ladybank Road, Mickleover,
Derbyshire DE3 5PF
Mansfield fans

And Smith Must Score
88 Friars Oak Road, Hassocks,
West Sussex BN6 8PY
Brighton and Hove Albion fans

An Imperfect Match
80 Stapleton Hall Road,
London N4 4QA
Arsenal fans/general European football

Another Bloody Sunday
42 Armley Lodge Road, Armley,
Leeds LS12 2AT
Leeds Rugby League fans

Archie! Archie! What's The Score?
PO Box 642, Glasgow G11 7QL
General Scottish football

Arsenal Echo Echo
30 Dene Road, Guildford,
Surrey, GU1 4DD
Arsenal fans

Attack!
9 Elm Close, Loddon,
Norfolk NR14 6LG
Norwich City fans

AWOL
11a Forth Street, Edinburgh EH1 3LE
Meadowbank Thistle fans

Aye Monotonous
15 Barronscourt Terrace,
Edinburgh EH8 7EW
Hibs fans

Aye Aye Rhubarb Pie
21 Soaper Lane Shelf, South
Bradford BD6 3NP
Bradford Park Avenue 'fans'

Aye Ready
PO Box 356, Glasgow G44 4DW
Rangers fans

Bad
90J St George's Drive,
London SW1V 4DA
Birmingham City fans

Balls
6 Gray's Inn Buildings, Roseberry
Avenue, London EC1R 4PH
General football

The Banker Magazine
41a The Grove, Central Finchley,
London N3
Lincoln City fans

Bayview Bulletin
60 Rothes Road, Glenrothes,
Fife KY6 1BN
East Fife fans

Beachy's Head
20 Whybourne Crest, Tunbridge
Wells, Kent TN2 5BS
Tunbridge Wells fans

The Beanos
Tamano Braco, Dunblane FK15 9LP
Stirling Albion fans

Behind The Sticks
Unit 22B, 31 Aire Street,
Leeds LS1 4HT
General Rugby League

Bernard of the Bantams
83 North Road, Wibsey,
Bradford, West Yorkshire
Bradford City fans/general football

Better Red Than Dead
Old Lismona Fact, Shillington Street,
Portadown, Co Armagh
Portadown fans

Beyond the Boundary
Flat 2, 153 Coppice Street,
Werneth, Oldham
Oldham Athletic fans

Big One Hans!
67 Vernon Road, Chester CH1 4JT
Wimbledon fans

Bishop 3-1
70 Witton Street, Northwich, Cheshire
Witton Albion fans

Black and Red All Over
(changed name to
18 Hours From Rotterdam)
Man United fans

Black and White
PO Box 7, Gateshead NE8 1TA
Newcastle United fans

Bloomer Shoots, Shilton Saves
10 Quorn Rise, Sunnyhill, Derby
Derby County history

Blow Football
8 Beaumont Road, Bournville,
Birmingham B30 2DY
General football

The Blues Brothers
Flat 2, 81 Westbourne Park Road,
London W2 5QH
Chelsea, Linfield and Rangers fans

Blue and Wight
113a Whitepit Lane, Newport, IOW
Portsmouth fans

Blue For You
PO Box 51, Lisburn,
County Antrim BT27 5ND
Linfield fans

Blue Print
PO Box 44, Worsley,
Manchester M28 4TE
Man City fans

Bluenews
Spring Place, St Aubyns Close,
Orpington, Kent BR6 OSN
Croydon fans

Blue Wail
62 Liverpool Road, Crosby,
Merseyside L23 5SJ
Everton fans

Boardbuster
69 Helvellyn Avenue, Lambton,
Washington NE38 OQL
Newcastle United fans

Bobbing Along
2 Moy Road, Roath, Cardiff CF2 4SG
Cardiff City fans

Bob's Finger
8 Walshingham Gardens, Townhill
Park, Southampton SO2 2QD
Subbuteo fans

The Boleyn Scorcher
311 Lewis Buildings, Liverpool
Road, London N1 1LL
West Ham United fans

The Bonker
(merged with **Deranged Ferret**)
PO Box 1211, London N3 1RF
Lincoln City fans

Born Kicking
4 High Sandgrove, Cleadon,
Sunderland SR6 7RW
Women who love football

The Boys Done Well
11 Corrennie Gardens,
Edinburgh EH10 6DG
Hearts fans

Boy's Own
London
Football/music fans

The Bounty Hunter
PO Box 576, Bristol BS99 1QJ
Bristol City fans

Brian Moore's Head Looks
Uncannily Like London Planetarium
9 Knight Avenue, Gillingham,
Kent ME7 1UE
Gillingham fans/general Kent football

Bring The Noise
10 Devon Road, Swindon SN2 1PQ
Swindon Town fans

The Bureau
172 Leytonstone Road,
London E15 1LH
Non League fans

The Butfie
4 Treebank Square, Kilwinning,
Scotland
Kilwinning Rangers fans

The Bugle
AKA Books and Comics, 33 Virginia
Street, Glasgow G1 1TU
Morton fans

Buzztalk
4 Seymour Road, London N3 2NH
Barnet fans

Calling All Comrades
50 Rashee road, Ballyclare,
Co Antrim BT39 9HP
Ballyclare Comrades fans

Capital Gills
43 Fox Street, Gillingham, Kent
Gillingham fans

The Cappielow Bugle
AKA Books and Comics, 33 Virginia
Street, Glasgow G1 1TU
Morton fans

The Casbah
Cliftonville fans

Carlton, Carlton
Flat 3, 43 Gwendolen Avenue, Putney,
London SW15 6EP
Wimbledon fans

CAT
62 Broadmeadow, Fatfield,
Washington NE38 8RH
Sunderland fans

The Celt
7 Clayton Terrace, Glasgow G31 2JA
Celtic fans

Celtic United News
79 Sedgeborough Road,
Manchester M16 7EL
Celtic/Man United fans

Central Heating
9 How Street, Bretonside, Plymouth
Plymouth Argyle fans

Chairboys Gas
Cedar Cottage, Green End Road,
Radnage, High Wycombe HP14 4BZ
Wycombe Wanderers fans

Champion Hill Street Blues
106 Wolverton, Alvey Street,
Walworth, London SE127 2AF
Dulwich Hamlet fans

Cheat
31 Westbrook Road, Chapeltown,
Sheffield S30 4YE
Sheffield Wednesday fans

Chelsea Collector
5 St Matthews Drive, Borstal,
Rochester ME31 3NW
Chelsea fans

Chelsea Independent
PO Box 459, London E7 8LU
Chelsea fans

The Citizen
53 Newton Park, Newton Street,
Faiths, Norwich NR10 3LR
Norwich City fans

The Cityzen
Flat 4, 11 Cedar Road,
Norwich NR1 14L
Norwich City fans

The Cityzen
Manchester City FC Supporters Club,
Maine Road, Manchester
Man City fans

City Gent
46 Ainsty Road, Wetherby LS22 4QS
Bradford City fans

Clap Your Hands Stamp Your Feet
25 Chestnut Drive, Pinner,
Middlesex HA5 1LX
Watford fans

The Cockney Latic
86 Martland Mill Lane, Wigan,
Lancashire
Wigan Athletic fans

Come On Dagenham
Use Your Forwards
12 Deva House, White Hart Lane,
Collier Row, Romford, Essex
Dagenham fans

Crazy House
Top Floor Studios, 27-29 Union Street,
London SE1
General football

The Cricketer's Anorak
17-24 St Johns Mansions,
London E5 8HT
General cricket

The Crooked Spireite
Flat 3, 119 Newbold Road,
Chesterfield S41 7PS
Chesterfield fans

Cross Rhodes
36 Wetherfield, Stanstead,
Essex CM24 8JB
Bishop Stortford fans

Crossbar
12 Belle Vue Terrace, Guiseley,
Leeds LS20 9BU
Leeds United fans

Crying Time Again
Bay Horse, 39 Bothwell Road, Hamilton
Hamilton Academicals

The Cumberland Sausage
53 Yewdale Road, Carlisle,
Cumbria CA2 7SN
Carlisle United fans

Dagger Magazine
3 Westhill, Stantonbury, Milton
Keynes MK4 6BG
Dagenham fans

The Dalymount Roar
PO Box 2932, Phibsborough, Dublin 7
Bohemian fans

Dear John
89 Thornwood Drive, Broomhill,
Glasgow G11
Partick Thistle fans

Dens Scene
47 Malcolm's Mount, Stonehaven,
Kincardineshire AB3 2SR
Dundee fans

De-Pleated
93 Jeans Way, Dunstable LU5 4PR
Luton Town fans

Deranged Ferret
(merged with **The Bonker**)
30 Church Meadow, Alpington,
Norwich NR14 7NY
Lincoln City fans

Derry Rumba
PO Box 3, Broughty Ferry DD5 2YG
Dundee fans

Devalued
2 Lincoln Road, Failsworth,
Manchester M35 0GN
Southampton fans

Dial M For Merthyr
9 Linden Way, Trefechan, Merthyr
Tydfil CF48 2EL
Merthyr Tydfil fans

The Director
47 Rainford Road, Billinge,
Wigan WN5 7PG
St Helens Rugby League fans

The Donkey's Tale
43 Fox Street, Gillingham,
Kent ME7 1HH
Gillingham fans

Dons Outlook
34 Alexandra Road, London SW19 7SZ
Wimbledon fans

Don't Get Sucked In
17 Knipersley Road, Wylde Green,
Sutton Coldfield B73 5JT
Sunday League fans

Don't Just Stand There
12 Gresham Road, Derby,
Derbyshire
General football in East Midlands

Don't Panic
106 Birchanger Road, South Norwood,
London SE25 5BG
General football in London

Down The Lane
2 Toynbec Close, Chislehurst,
Kent BR7 6TH
Bromley fans

Dribble
117 Maldon Road, Colchester,
Essex CO3 3AX
Ipswich Town fans

The Drop
40 Pickhurst Lane, Bromley,
Kent BR2 7J
Charlton Athletic/Crystal Palace fans

Dwy Droed Chwith
Encil Coed, Plasgwyn, Pwlheli,
Gwynedd LL53 6UA
General football (Welsh language)

Each Game As It Comes
79 Harlow Crescent, Harrogate,
Yorkshire HG2 0AY
General football

Eagle Eye
30 Manor Court, York Way,
Whetstone, London N20 0DR
Crystal Palace fans

East End Connection
54 Chaucer Road, Herne Hill,
London SE24 7JB
West Ham United fans

Editors Foot
26 Salisbury Close, Tonbridge, Kent
Tonbridge fans

Electric Blue
Man City fans

Elfmeter
34 Oaklands Avenue, Harbone,
Birmingham B17 9TY
General German football

Elm Park Disease
PO Box 51, Reading RG1 7JB
Reading fans

The Elmslie Ender
37 Grange Road, Kentonm Harrow,
Middlesex HA1 2PR
Wealdstone fans

The End
General football/music fans

The Evergreen
PO Box 151, Plymouth PL1 1FT
Plymouth fans

European Football
11 Cotton House, Thames Street,
London SE10 9DG
General European football

Every Man A Football Artist
75 John Street, Kilkenny
Kilkenny City fans

The Exe-Directory
PO Box 106, Exeter
Exeter City fans

A DON'T COME FO' THE FOOTY, A COME FO' THE FASHION ... ME.

The Falkirk Unofficial Fanzine
2 Rose Terrace,
Stenhousemuir FK5 4DW
Falkirk fans

Fanzine Classics
54 Chaucer Road, Herne Hill,
London SE24 0NU
General Football

53 Miles West of Venus
206 South Meadow Lane, Broadgate,
Preston PR1 8JP
PNE fans

Flickin 'n' Kickin
7 Loughborough Road, Burton-on-the-
Wolds, Loughborough, Leics LE12
Notts County and Subbuteo fans

The Final Hurdle
PO Box 91, Dundee DD1 9DW
Dundee United fans

Fingerpost
2 Oak Close, Tipton, Staffs DY4 0AY
WBA fans

Five to Three
Encil Y Coed, Plasgwyn, Pwllheli,
Gwynedd LL53 6UA
General football (esp Welsh clubs)

Flag Edge Touch
19 Staines Close, Grasby Road, Hull
Hull KR Rugby League fans

Flashing Blade
85 Charnley Avenue, Sheffield S11
Sheffield United fans

**Flippin' Heck Ref,
That Was A Foul Surely**
268 Somers Road North, Fratton,
Portsmouth PO1 1PL
Waterlooville fans

Floodlight
8 Maple Drive, Kirby Cross,
Frinton-on-Sea, Essex
Colchester United fans

THE FALKIRK UNOFFICIAL FANZINE No.7

40p

MOTHERWELLS COLIN O'NEILL FINDS HE IS NOT VERY POPULAR AMONGST FALKIRK SUPPORTERS AFTER OUR RECENT CUP EXIT.

Fly Me To The Moon
14 Selkirk Close, Saltersgill,
Middlesbrough, Cleveland
Middlesbrough fans

Follow Your Instinct
6 Queens Gate, Lipson, Plymouth,
Devon PL4 7PW
Halesowen Town fans

Follow Follow
PO Box 539, Glasgow G11 7LT
Rangers fans

Follow The Yellow Brick Road
35 Stoneyford Road, Sutton-in-
Ashfield, Notts NG17 4DA
Mansfield fans

Football and Fiesta
62 Queensgate, Bolton, Lancashire
General European football

The Football Pink
529 Charles Barry Crescent, Hulme,
Manchester M15 5DL
Gay and Lesbian football supporters

Football Supporter
PO Box 11, Liverpool L26 1XP
General football (FSA)

Football Utopia
Spring Place, St Aubyns Close,
Orpington, Kent BR6 0SN
General football in South East London

Footie
PO Box 664, London SW11 6AL
General football

So you're the new Y.T.S. Trainer? I think I'd like to explain one or two little things, first...

Russell ★ Grant FORECAST

Time to cast a dubious gaze into Russell's crystal football....(don't all rush to the bookies at once now!)

SCOTTISH CUP WINNERS: Celtic.
SKOL CUP WINNERS: Aberdeen.
PREMIER DIVISION CHAMPIONS: Rangers.
Runners-up: Celtic.
Relegated: St.Mirren (phew!!).
FIRST DIVISION CHAMPIONS: Partick Thistle.
Runners-up: Dundee.
Relegated: Brechin City and Clyde.
SECOND DIVISION CHAMPIONS: Stirling Albion.
Runners-up: Albion Rovers.

Fortune's Always Hiding
16 Clifton Mansions, Cold Harbour
Lane, London SW9 8EL
West Ham United fans

Foul
Cambridge
General football

Foul (incorporating the **Mousse**)
72 Francis Avenue, Southsea, Hants
Waterlooville fans

The Foundation Stone
PO Box 164, Sevenoaks,
Kent TN13 3QW
Maidstone United fans

482 Days
33 Oxford Road, Cowley,
Oxford OX4 2EN
General British ice hockey

4000 Holes
PO Box 609, Ribchester, Preston,
Lancs PR3 3YT
Blackburn Rovers fans

4-1
8 Maple Place, Kilmarnock
Ayr United fans

The Fox
36 Main Street, Huncote,
Leicester LE9 6AU
Leicester City fans

Frattonize
PO Box 122, Southsea PO4 9UL
Portsmouth fans

Freakscene
PO Box 559, Glasgow G43 1EG
Dundee United fans

Friday Night Fever
38 Stanton Drive, Upton,
Chester CH2 2JF
Tranmere Rovers fans

From Behind Your Fences
82 Osprey Road,
Biggleswade SG18 8HE
Boston United fans

From Home to Home
61-2 Amiens Street, Dublin 1
Shelbourne fans

From Hull To Eternity
Spring House, Seaside Road, Easington,
Hull HU12 0TY
Hull City fans

Fulton 1-0
PO Box 575, Glasgow G11 7QH
Pollock Juniors fans

The Gashead
30 Co-Operation Road, Green Bank,
Bristol
Bristol Rovers fans

Gatecrashing
32 Yarrow Close, Broadstairs,
Kent CT10 1PW
Margate fans

Get A Grip Ref
1 Maltby Road, Scunthorpe DN17 2JD
Scunthorpe United fans

The Gibbering Clairvoyant
95 Geils Avenue, Dumbarton
Dumbarton fans

Give 'Em Beans
5 Ramsden Square, Duke Street,
Barrow, Cumbria
Barrow fans

Glass Routes
78 Meriden Avenue, Wollaston,
Stourbridge DY8 4QS
Stourbridge fans

Glenmalure Gazette
PO Box 2443, Dublin 17
Shamrock Rovers fans

The Globe
PO Box 395, Cambridge CB1 3LT
General football/music fans

Golden Days
Flat 3, Tiverton, Devon EX16 6AW
Maidstone United fans

The Good, the Bad and the Ugly
37 Swanston Drive,
Edinburgh EH10 7BP
Hearts fans

The Gooner
Twiga, St Aubuyns Gardens,
Orpington, Kent BR6 0SW
Arsenal fans

Gorgie Wave
11 Corenie Gardens,
Edinburgh EH10 6DG
Hearts fans

Grapevine
Club Shop, Wimbledon FC,
49 Durnsford Road, London SW19
Wimbledon fans

The Greatest City
12 Swallow Close, Havant,
Hampshire PO9 2RA
Portsmouth fans

Great Easter
14 South Trinity Road, Edinburgh
Scottish Rugby Union fans

The Greatest Game
PO Box 1895, 52 Call Lane,
Leeds LS1 6DT
The Voice of the Rugby League Supporters
Association

(A Travellers Guide to) Greek Football
87 St John's Park, Blackheath,
London SE3 7JW
General Greek football

The Green Piece
PO Box 112, Plymouth PL1 1DR
Plymouth Argyle fans

Grorty Dick
7 Ruth Close, Tipton, Staffs DY4 0AR
WBA fans

Ground Hopper
Flat 1, 64 Hunting Gate Drive,
Chessington, Surrey KT9 2DD
Non League fans

Gull's Eye
57 Lydhurst Road, Worthing,
West Sussex
Brighton and Hove Albion fans

Gunflash
Arsenal Football Supporters Club,
Highbury, London
Arsenal fans

Hail Hail
92 Commerce Street, Glasgow G5
Celtic fans

Hail Mary
237 Wendover Road, Aylesbury,
Bucks HP21 9PB
American Football fans

Half Past Four And We're Two Down
Eassie House, Glamis, Forfar DD8 1SG
Dundee fans

The Hand of God
237 Wendover Road, Aylesbury,
Bucks HP21 9PB
England national team fans

The Hanging Sheep
41 Woodhall Terrace, Thornbury,
Bradford BD3 7BZ
Leeds United fans

Hardaker Rides Again
96 Repton Road, Brislington,
Bristol BS24 3LX
General football

Hearts (Stat) Attack
71 Deanburn Park,
Linlithgow EH49 6HA
Hearts fans

Head The Ball
PO Box 2466, Dublin 8
General football Irish League

Hello Albert
39 Dalebrook Road, Sale,
Cheshire M33 3LD
Chester City fans

He's Not Danny Grady
Crewe Alexandra fans

Heart Beat
24 Mountbatten Close, Whitefield,
Manchester
Hearts fans

Hearts Review
12 Mavisbank, Loanhead,
Midlothian EH20 9DD
Hearts fans

The Hearts Supporter
46 Snaefell Avenue, Burnside,
Glasgow G73 5BL
Hearts fans

The Normid Nomad
An independent view of Bolton Wanderers
VOL 2 N° 3 NOVEMBER 1989 MONTHLY

The Hearts Supporter
PO Box 427, Edinburgh EH11 1RZ
Hearts fans

Heroes and Villains
PO Box 1703, Perry Barr,
Birmingham B42 1UZ
Aston Villa fans

Hibees Here, Hibees There
PO Box 611, London SW14 8QU
Hibs fans

Hibs Monthly
59 Comely Bank Road, Edinburgh
Hibs fans

Hibs OK?
68 Kelvin Drive, Maryhill,
Glasgow G20 8QN
Hibs fans

Hit The Bar
10 Grafton Street, Blackpool
General football (esp North West)

House of Pain
183 Liverpool Road, Great Sankey,
Warrington WA5 1QU
Warrington Rugbhy League fans

Hull, Hell and Happiness
119 North Road, Withernsea,
Hull HU9 2AX
Hull City fans

In Defence
43 Anglesey Road, Ponders End,
Enfield EN1 4HZ
Enfield fans

LIVERPOOL'S FANCY DRESS PARTY 1989

THIRD, JOHN BARNES AS A KU KLUX KLAN MAN
SECOND, BRUCE GROBBELAAR IN HIS ARMY GEAR
BUT THE WINNER IS, BAZZA AS AN ENGLAND PLAYER!!

It's Redford v soccer

CINEMA bosses aim to "score" with women abandoned by their soccer-mad men during the World Cup. Wives and girlfriends are being asked to name which movie heart throbs they want to see on screen while their fellas are at home glued to the TV. A spokesman for the six-cinema complex at High Wycombe, Bucks, said: "We will show films for ladies who can't stand football. "They can come with their girlfriends. "If they want Mel Gibson, Redford or Newman we will do our best to deliver."

Interesting Very Interesting
Solar Press, 6 Brackenfield Road,
Wessington, Derbyshire
Derby County fans

In The City
31 Ryemoor Road, Haxby,
York Y03 8GX
York City fans

In The Loft
24 Woodman Road, Catford,
London SE6 2SD
QPR fans

Intifada
14 Conway Road, Pontcanna,
Cardiff CF1 8NT
Cardiff City fans

In Touch
38 Bran, Acrefair, Wrexham,
Clwyd LL14 3HD
North Wales and West Cheshire FSA

Is It Red
Morton House, North Mossley Hill
Road, Liverpool L18
General football

Its Grim Up North
41 Gosforth Road, Blackpool FY2 9TP
General football

The Ivor Thirst Good Pub Guide
61 Stratford Road, West Brigford,
Nottingham NG2 6AZ
General football

Jackmail
38 Church Road, Baglan, Port Talbot,
West Glamorgan SA13 1QN
Swansea City fans

The Jag Mag
17 Popular Way, Masonhill, Ayr,
Scotland KA7 3PQ
East Kilbride Thistle fans

The Jam Piece
43 Polwarth Crescent, Edinburgh
Hearts fans

John Wilkins – On The Wagon
30 Stirling Way, Ramsgate,
Kent GT12 6NA
Margate fans

Jihad
29a Heath Street, London NW3 6TR
General football

Jim's Bald Head
44 Shafto Street, Rosehill,
Wallsend NE28 7AH
Newcastle United fans

The Johnny Flood Experience
48 Windyedge Crescent, Glasgow,
Scotland G13 1YF
Partick Thistle fans

Johnny Miller 96 Not Out?
10 Kirkstall Close, Eastbourne,
Sussex BN22 0UQ
General cricket

The Jolly Green Giant
4 Roscoe Crescent, Weston Point,
Runcorn, Cheshire WA7 4ES
Runcorn fans

The Jolly Potter
PO Box 257, 22 Call Lane,
Leeds LS1 6DT
Stoke City fans

Jungle Drums
PO Box 726, East Kilbride
Celtic fans

Junk Mail
17 Cavendish Grove,
Southampton SO1 2LE
Southampton fans

OPPOSITE
Attila The Stockbroker
Bury, March 91.

61

THIS EDITION: THE HIDEOUS GORDON McKEAG HORROR MASK... CENTRE PAGES...BILLY BRAMBLES...JIM'S JOVIALITIES... GOALS!...MEMORY !ATCH...!EMORY !ESS...AND !UCH !ORE!

Just Another Wednesday
52 Ullswater Road, Handforth,
Wilmslow, Cheshire SK9 3NQ
Sheffield Wednesday fans

Just One More Lap
8 Bramley Parade, Bowesfield Lane,
Stockton-on-Tees TS18 3TG
General speedway

A Kick Up The R's
6 Mill Cottages, Grindley Brook,
Nr Whitchurch, Shropshire
QPR fans

Killie Ken
34 Boyd Orr Crescent, Kilmaurs,
Kilmarnock KA3 2QB
Kilmarnock fans

King of the Kippax
25 Holdenbrook Close, Leigh,
Greater Manchester
Man City fans

The Lad Done Brilliant
Room 43, Wigram House, Ashley
Gardens, London SW1 1HH
General football

The Lancaster Town and City Historian
108 Hillend Crescent, Clarkson,
Glasgow G76 7XY
Lancaster City fans

A Large Scotch
15 York Road, Harescott Grange,
Shrewsbury SY1 3RD
Shrewsbury Town fans

North Bank Norman's
Did you know?
THAT TONY GALE THROWS UP BEFORE EVERY GAME TO MAKE SURE HE'S PLAYING ON AN EMPTY STOMACH!

Semper Te Fallant

GRORTY DICK

The Last Line Of Defence
19 Blantrye Street, Bishopmill, Elgin,
Moray, Scotland
Elgin City fans

Le Chic
16 South Hince Avenue, Glasgow,
Scotland G14 0QH
Clydebank fans

Les Bence-Manager's Notes
5 Clarks Place, Trowbridge,
Wiltshire BA14 7HA
Non League fans

Lennie Lawrence
433 Woodham Lane, Weybridge,
Surrey KT15 3QE
Charlton Athletic fans

Leyton Orientear
1 York Road, Leyton, London E10 5QE
Leyton Orient fans

Libero
58 Arundel Terrace,
London SW13 9DS
General Italian football

Light At The End of The Tunnel
19 The Terraces, Dartford,
Kent DA2 6BX
Dartford fans

The Lion Roars
24 Woodham Road, Catford,
London SE6 2SD
Millwall fans

Liverpool Are On The Tele Again
618 Dereham Road, Norwich,
Norfolk NR5 8TE
Norwich City fans

A Load of Bull
PO Box 277, 52 Call Lane,
Leeds LS1 6DT
Wolves fans

A Load of Cobbolds
62 Raynham Road, Bury St Edmunds,
Suffolk IP32 6ED
Ipswich Town fans

The Loiner
15 Richmond Hill Close,
Leeds LS9 8JU
Leeds Rugby League fans

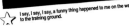

HAVE YOU HEARD THE ONE ABOUT THE NUMBER NINE...?

I say, I say, I say, a funny thing happened to me on the way to the training ground.

Long Ball Down The Middle
50 Hartington Close, Sudbury Hill,
Harrow, Middlesex HA1 3RL
Wealdstone fans

The Loonatic
25 Prince of Wales Avenue, Reading,
Berks R63 2UH
Forfar Athletic fans

A Love Supreme
PO Box 25, Newcastle-upon-Tyne,
Cleveland NE6 1QE
Sunderland fans

Love Street Syndrome
PO Box 27, Helensburgh,
Dumbartonshire G84 7EF
Saint Mirren fans

LYAL
27 Glenburren Park, Tuam Road,
Galway
Limerick fans

The Mad Axeman
10 Yealand Drive, Lancaster LA1 4EW
Lancaster City fans

Mad As A Hatter
30 Linden Road, Dunstable LU5 4NZ
Luton Town fans

The Mag
Unit 11, 25 Low Friar Street,
Newcastle-upon-Tyne NE1 5UE
Newcastle United fans

The Magic Sponge
Unit 22b, 31 Aire Street,
Leeds LS1 4HT
General football

Manchester Wolves
49 Kensington Drive, Bury BL8 2DE
Wolverhampton Wanderers fans

Many Miles From Home
66 Glanville Park, London SE13 7DX
Blackburn Rovers fans

Marching Altogether
Leeds TOC Club, Saville Mount, Leeds
Leeds United fans

Maybe Its Because
29 Parkdale Road, Plumstead,
London SE18
General Football

Medalion Atkinson
27 Tennyson Street, Lincoln, LN1 1LZ
Sheffield Wednesday fans

The Memoirs of Seth Bottomley
PO Box 418, Longton, Stoke-on-Trent,
Staffs ST3 6SB
Port Vale fans

Mighty Quinn
27 Laburnum Avenue, Heworth,
Gateshead NE10 8HH
Newcastle United fans

The Mill on the Maun
8 Chestnut Drive, Mansfield,
Notts NG18 4PW
Mansfield Town fans

Millerntor Roar
Beim Grunen Jageri,
2000 Hamburg 36, Germany
St Pauli fans

Mission Impossible
8 Bramley Parade, Bowesfield Lane,
Stockton-on-Tees TS18 3JG
Darlington fans

Mission Terminated
14 Conway Road, Paignton TQ4 5LF
Torquay United fans

Mi Whippet's Dead
11 Apsley Street, Middlesbrough
Rotherham United fans

Mo Mo Super Mo
PO Box 3, Broughty Fery,
Dundee DD5 2YG
Montrose fans

The Moon
PO Box 20, 1 Nelson Street, Leicester
Leicester City fans

More Money Than Sense
5 Meuthen Road, Eastney,
Portsmouth PO4 9UL
Portsmouth fans

More Than A Game
56 Springdale Road, Broadstone,
Dorset BH18 9BX
General football

Mud, Sweat and Beers
PO Box 436, Hemel Hempstead,
Herts HP3 8UF
Watford fans

Mug Punter
PO Box 117,
Belfast BT1 1AA
General horse racing

Murphy's Frog
46 Long Mynd Avenue, Up Hatterley,
Cheltenham GL 15 5QN
Non League fans

My Eyes Have Seen The Glory
PO Box 844, London E16 4HE
Tottenham Hotspur fans

The Name of The Rose
PO Box 19 (SEPDO),
Manchester M12 5RZ
Lancashire cricket fans

The Nearly Men
Widnes Rugby League fans

Never Mind The Boleyn
19 Canada Road, Acton,
London W3 0NP
West Ham United fans

Never Mind The Boys End
Middlesbrough fans

Never Mind The Danger
77 Beulah Road, Walthamstow,
London E17 9LD
Norwich City fans

Never Say Dai
11 Augustan Drive, Caerlon,
Gwent NP6 1DD
Newport Town fans

NHS No Home Stadium
43 Hunters Road, Chessington,
Surrey KT9 1RU
Kingstonian fans

A Nightmare on Dee Street
30 Chamberlain Street,
Belfast BT5
Glentoran fans

The Nine 'Oilers
Dewsbury Rugby League

9½ Months
8 Salehurst Road, Brockley,
London SE4
Bristol Rovers fans

NI Soccer
152 Albertbridge Road,
Belfast BT5 4GS
General Northern Ireland football

The 92nd Club
32 Moybray Street, Castleton,
Rochdale OL11 3JF
Rochdale fans

Nobody Will Ever Know
219 Portland Place, South Tottenham,
London N15 4SZ
Swansea City fans

No Idle Talk
71 Deanburn Park,
Linlithgow EH49 6HA
Hearts fans

No One Likes Us
WBNC Media, Herbrand Street,
London WC1 1LB
Millwall fans

Non League Football Fanfare
26 Orchard Road, Kingston-upon-
Thames, Surrey KT1 2QW
Non League fans

Non League Traveller
Top O The Bank, Evesham Road,
Broadway, Worcs WR12 7DG
Non League fans

No Nay Never
PO Box 999, Nelson, Lancashire
Burnley fans

The Normid Nomad
15 Acresfield, Adlington, Chorley,
Lancs PR7 4JZ
Bolton Wanderers fans

64

The North East Hibernian
Moray Tait, Aberdeen University SU,
Aberdeen AB1 1BA
Hibs fans

The Northern Light
PO Box 269, Aberdeen AB9 8EN
Aberdeen fans

The North Stand Blues
60 Ashfield Park Drive, Standish,
Wigan WN6 0EG
Chorley Town fans

Not An Official Programme
Fulham rugby league fans

Not The 8502
56 Springdale Road,
Broadstone, Dorset
Bournemouth fans

Not The View
PO Box 306, Glasgow G21 2EA
Celtic fans

A Novel School of Thought
93 Kingsley Way, London N2 0EL
General football

O Bluebird of Happiness
96 LLandaff Road, Canton,
Cardiff CF1 9NN
Cardiff City fans

The Oatcake
PO Box 276, Stoke-on-Trent ST1 5RU
Stoke City fans

The Occasional Terrorist
39 Longlands Court, Spring Grove,
Mitcham, Surrey CR4 2NQ
Tooting and Mitcham fans

Oh Yes This Boy Can Wait!
General music and football

Offside Trap
66 Westlands Road, Hull HU5 5ND
General football

Off The Ball
Birmingham
General football

Off The Junction
Aston Villa fans

Off The Shelf
PO Box 1547, Highbury,
London N5 1LJ
Tottenham Hotspur fans

Old McDiarmid Had A Farm
103 Hillhouse Road,
Edinburgh EH4 7AD
St Johnstone fans

(On A) Life Support Machine
c/o Muirtown Motel Bar,
Clachnaharry Road, Inverness
Caledonian fans

On A Wing and A Prayer
10 Harvell Court, Harvell Crescent,
London SE2 0PS
Welling United fans

Once A Tim
PO Box 759, Glasgow G41 3AR
Celtic fans

Once Upon a Tyne
14 Hertford Close, Whitley Bay,
Tyne and Wear NE25 9XH
Newcastle United fans

On Cloud Seven
104 Dungevan Road, Hull HU8 9LF
Hull City fans

One Minute To Go
News Gallery, 38 Liverpool Road,
Lydiate, Lancs
Liverpool fans

One-Nil Down Two-One Up
71a Hillfield Park, London N10 3QU
Arsenal fans

One Team in Bristol
Bristol City Supporters Club, Bristol
Bristol City fans

One Team in Dundee
PO Box 1909, 11a Forth Street,
Edinburgh EH1 3LE
Dundee United fans

One Team in Glasgow
PO Box 5, Erskine, Renfrewshire
Partick Thistle fans

One Team in Ulster
9 Belvoir Park, Lisburn,
Co Antrim BT28 1TZ
Linfield fans

Only The Lonely
6 Ossian Road, Newlands,
Glasgow G43 2JJ
Aidrieonians fans

On The Terraces
PO Box 1511, London NW1 6RY
West Ham United fans

On The March
21 Mon Crescent, Bitterne,
Southampton S02 5QW
Southampton fans

On The One Road
10 Mendip Way, Highfield, Hemel
Hempstead HP2 5QY
General Irish football

Ooh Gary Gary
Barbara Ellen, NME, IPC Towers,
Stamford Street, London SE1
Gary Lineker fans

Ooh I Think Its My Groin
42a Graham Road, Mitcham, Surrey
QPR fans

Our Day Will Come
PO Box 158, Doncaster DN1 2RS
Man United/Celtic fans

Out Of Court
Flat 3, High Point, 50 Midanbury Lane,
Southampton S02 4HF
Bournemouth fans

Over Land and Sea
PO Box 26, Dagenham,
Essex RM10 8XY
West Ham United fans

Over The Gate
PO Box 759, Bristol BS99 1ZP
Bristol City fans

Over The Wall
16a Truro Road, Woodgreen,
London N22 4EL
Albion Rovers fans

Paper Roses
12 MacCallum Place, Kilmarnock
Kilmarnock fans

The Peacock
Box 442, Sheffield S1 3UN
Leeds United fans

The Peterborough Effect
PO Box 16, Huntingdon,
Cambs PE18 6NH
Peterborough United fans

The Pie
61 Statford Road, West Bridgeford,
Nottingham NG2 6AZ
Notts County fans

Pie In The Sky
102 Lowfield Road, Caversham
Park Village, Reading
Nentori Padwits fans

Pie Eaters Prescription
22 Greenland Avenue, Standish,
Wigan WN6 0TH
Wigan Rugby League fans

Pigskins 'n' Peachtrees
24 Pollards Hill, London SW16 4LN
Atlanta Falcons fans

The Playboy
15 Anderson Crescent, Bishopmill,
Elgin IV30 2HJ
Elgin City fans

The PNE View
PNE fans

Poppies At The Gates of Dawn
Patgod Towers, 8 Pikes End, Pinner,
Middlesex HA5 2EX
Kettering Town fans

Preston Other Paper
PO Box 172, Preston PR1 4BU
PNE fanzine with Issue 8, October 1989

Pretty In Pink
S6 Hardy Farm, Hardy Lane, Chorlton-
Cum-Hardy, Manchester M21
Brighton and Hove Albion fans

Pride and Passion
PO Box 2807, Dublin
Rep of Ireland national team fans

Pride of the South
Top Floor Flat, 3 Church Road,
Lower Parkstone, Poole, Dorset
General football (esp South of England)

Notts County Fanzine

40p

THE TONER

N°1

'A Haircut and a ...'

Punt
28 Springhill Gardens, Shawlands,
Glasgow, Scotland
General Scottish football

The Punter
62 Kelvingrove Street, Glasgow,
Scotland G3 7SA
General Scottish football

Psycho Arab
31 McBain Place, Kinross, Tayside
Dundee United fans

Pyramid Football
PO Box 553, London N2 8LJ
Non League fans

Que Sera Sera
PO Box 202, Glasgow G12 8EQ
Scotland national team fans

Racing Ghost
Flat 3, 53 Camden Park Road, Camden
Town, London NW1 9BH
Horse racing fans

Raging Bull
8 Nixon Road, Oxford 0X4 4BU
Oxford United fans

Rah! Rah! Rah!
283 Campkin Road, Cambridge CB4 2LD
Cambridge United fans

Raise The Roof
3 The Hawthorns, Wykegate Road,
Thorne, Doncaster DN8 5PE
Doncaster Rovers fans

Rangers Historian
21 Cornaig Road, Glasgow G53 5AW
Rangers fans

Rebels Without A Clue
62 Stoke Poges Lane, Slough, Berks
Slough Town fans

Rebel Yell
52 Call Lane, Leeds LS1 6DT
Castleford Rugby League fans

Reclaim The Game
59 Oakwood Road, Halewood,
Liverpool L26 1XD
Original national newsletter of FSA

The Red Card
42 Hillside Close, Barvstead,
Surrey SM7 1ET
Chelsea fans

Red Issue
PO Box 16, Urmston,
Manchester M31 1LX
Man United fans

Red News
PO Box 384, London WC1N 3RJ
Man United fans

Reliant Robin
38 Bran, Acrefair, Wrexham,
Clwyd LL14 3HD
Wrexham fans

Resign Roberts Re-Sign
488 London Road, Davenham,
Northwich, Cheshire CW9 8HW
Northwich Victoria fans

The Robin
2 Clarence Court, Clarence Road,
Cheltenham GL52 2AX
Cheltenham Town fans

Rodney Rodney
PO Box 19 (SEPDO),
Manchester M12 5RZ
General football (esp North West)

Roger Connel's Beard
88 Farm Road, Morden,
Surrey, SM4 6RB
Wimbledon fans

Roker Roar
PO Box 19, Sunderland SR1 1BT
Sunderland fans

Roll on 4:40
63 Ambrose Rise, Dedridge,
Livingston, West Lothian EH54 6JT
Meadowbank Thistle fans

Roots Hall Roar
25 Southbourne Grove, Westcliff-
on-Sea, Essex S50 9UW
Southend United fans

Roots Hall Ramblings
2 Burdett Avenue, Westcliff-on-Sea,
Essex S50 7JW
Southend United fans

Rub Of The Greens
59a Springfield Road, New Southgate,
London N11 1RL
Plymouth Argyle fans

Russians Roulette
22 Queen Street, Rushden,
Northants NN10 0AZ
Rushden Town fans

Saddle Sore
24 Blenheim Road, Horspath,
Oxford 0X9 1RY
Walsall fans

Scarborough Warning
1b Stepney Drive, Scarborough,
Yorks Y012 5DP
Scarborough fans

OPPOSITE
When Skies Are Grey seller
Goodison Park, May 91.

THE MEMOIRS OF
ETH BOTTOMLEY.

Schwarz Auf Weis
Postfach 113, 1070 Vienna, Austria
Wiener Sport-Club fans

Scoop John B
PO Box 183 Liverpool L69 7DH
General Rugby Union

Scottish Non League Review
12 Windsor Road, Renfrew PA4 0SS
Non League (Scotland)

Scottish Football Historian
14 Raith Crescent, Kircaldy,
Fife KY2 5NN
General Scottish football

Scottish 'Zine Scene
71 Deanburn Park, Linlithgow, West
Lothian EH49 6HA
General fanzines

Scrumbag
PO Box Swansea SA1 1EY
General Rugby Union

The Seasider
32a The Chase, Rayleigh,
Essex SS8 8QN
Southend United fans

The Shankill Skinhead
45 Merchant's Quay, Salford
Man United fans

The Sheep
PO Box 23, Alfreton, Derby DE55 4SL
Derby County fans

The Sheeping Giant
Tarren, Llangedwyn, Nr Oswestry,
Shropshire SY10 9LT
Wrexham fans

Shippo Shout
High Garth, Red Lane, Masham,
Nr Ripon HG4 4HH
York City fans

Shots In the Dark
PO Box 238, Guildford,
Surrey GU2 6FY
Aldershot fans

last seasons top 5 Drinking songs

Show Me The Way to Go Home
PO Box 180, Maidstone,
Kent ME16 8AN
Maidstone United fans

Shrimper's View
21 The Vineway, Dovercourt,
Harwich, Essex
Harwich and Parkstone fans

Simon's Haircut
129 Roberts Road, Aldershot, Hants
Farnborough Town fans

Sing When We're Fishing
27 Crowhill Avenue, Cleethorpes,
South Humberside DN35 8DF
Grimsby Town fans

Sing When We're Ploughin
73 Rickman Hill, Coulsdon,
Surrey CR5 3DT
Norwich City fans

Size 10½ Boots
10 Dollis Avenue, Finchley
London N3 1TX
Mansfield Town fans

The Sleeping Giant
96 Stahmore Street, Barnhill,
Dundee DD5 2NZ
Dundee fans

Someone Likes Us
73 Brixton Hill Court, Brixton Hill,
London SW2 1QY
Millwall fans

The Sound of the Shay
82 Alma Road, Ponders End,
Enfield EN3 4UQ
Halifax Town fans

Southender
1 Adstone Road, Belle Vale, Liverpool
South Liverpool fans

Southriding
4 Cope Street, Barnsley S70 4HY
Barnsley fans

The Spurs Screws
10 Cheltenham Gardens, Loughton,
Essex IG10 3AW
Tottenham Hotspur fans

Spud International
17 St Mary's Close, Attleborough,
Norfolk NR17 2ED
Norwich City fans

The Spur
153 Upton Road, Bexley Heath,
Kent DA6 8LY
Tottenham Hotspur fans

The Square Ball
Unit 22b, 31 Aire Street,
Leeds LS1 4HT
Leeds United fans

Start!
36 Hazelmere Road, St Albans,
Herts AL4 9RN
Music/Lancashire football fans

The Steam Pig
1512 Smithy Hill, Wisbey, Bradford
Bradford Northern Rugby League fans

Sticky Wicket
160 Halse Road, Brackley,
Northants NN13 6EG
General cricket

Still Mustn't Grumble
PO Box 310, Edinburgh EH9 1BU
Hearts fans

The Stockholmian
Tommy Backman, Agronomvagen 30,
183 47 Taby, Sweden
General Swedish football

Storming With Menace
11 Chatsworth Way, Carlyon Bay,
St Austell, Cornwall PL25 3SL
General football (esp Plymouth Argyle)

Suffer Little Children
358 Seaside, Eastbourne BN22 7RY
Crystal Palace fans

Swedish Football For English Readers
Joakim Sjoborg, Telegatan 6,
703 41 Orebro, Sweden
General Swedish football

SW6
PO Box 1005, London E6 2AY
Chelsea fans

The Tackler!
Unit 22b, 31 Aire Street,
Leeds LS1 4HT
General humour

Taking The Biscuit
5 Fetlock Close, Clapham,
Beds MK416BG
Reading fans

Tales From The Potting Shed
POBox 210, Fulwood, Preston PR2 4XF
PNE fans

Talking Bull
45 Knightswood, Hampton Dene,
Hereford
Hereford United fans

Talk of the Town End
20 Calder Close, Enfield EN1 3TS
Enfield fans

Tangerine Dream
29 Roseacre, Blackpool FY4 2PN
Blackpool/Chorley rugby fans

Tartan Esercito
11 Corennie Gardens,
Edinburgh EH10 6DG
Scotland national team fans

Tayside Football Review
45 Sutherland Crescent,
Dundee DD2 2HP
General Scottish football

Terrace Talk
7 Copper Beech Close, Dunnington,
York Y01 5PY
York City fans

There Is A Rat In The Camp
72 Telephone Road, Southsea,
Portsmouth, Hants
Brighton and Hove Albion fans

**There's A Store
Where The Creatures Meet**
14 Eildon Drive, Barrhead G78 2EA
St Mirren fans

There's Only One F in Fulham
37 Ember Lane, Esher,
Surrey KT10 8EA
Fulham fans

There's Only One Reggie Harris!
9 Annalee Gardens, South Ockendon,
Essex RM15 5DE
Aveley fans

The Thin Yellow Stripe
2 Norbett Road, Arnold, Notts NG5 8EB
Notts County fans

The Thistle
21 Little Road, Edinburgh EH16 6SH
Meadowbank Thistle fans

Those Were The Days
46 Smart Green, Cheshunt,
Herts EN7 6BA
Ipswich Town fans

Three In A Row
17 Mauchline Road, Auchinleck
Auchinleck Talbot fans

Through The Wind and Rain
PO Box 23, Bootle L30 2SA
Liverpool fans

Tiger Roar
70 Sussex Gardens, Hucclecote,
Gloucester GL3 3SU
Gloucester City fans

Tired and Weary
113 Longmore Road, Shirley,
Solihull B90 3EF
Birmingham City fans

Tomato Soup and Lentils
33 John Street, Arbroath,
Angus DD11 1BT
Leeds United/Arbroath fans

Tooting Tearaways
28 Bruce Road, Mitcham,
Surrey CR4 2BG
Tooting/Mitcham fans

Town
PO Box 375, Luton LU1 4QP
Luton Town fans

The Trent Times
38 Brendon Road, Woolaton,
Nottingham NG8 1HZ
Nottingham Forest fans

The Tricky Tree
Gordon Square, West Bridgford,
Nottingham NG2 5UP
Nottingham Forest fans

SIZE 10½ BOOTS
THE VOICE OF STAGS OUTSIDE NOTTS

'size 10½' sales team drink profits of last issue

NO. 8
NOV/ DEC '89
40 P

THE FARM On The Ball Boys —AARGH!

ONE MINUTE TO GO LADS

I WANT CANDY

PULL

STEVE McMAHON

The Trotter
18a Hogarth Court, Steeplands,
Bushey, Herts WD2 3EP
Bolton Wanderers fans

True Blues Magazine
102 Lifestan Way, Thorpe Bay, Essex
Southend United fans

Try Try Try
4 Linley Road, Pemberton,
Wigan WN5 9ES
Wigan Rugby League fans

Two For Joy
60 Ashfield Drive, Standish,
Wigan WN6 0EG
Chorley fans

Two Left Feet
Flat 8, Y Dwnan South Beach, Pwllheli,
Gwynedd LL53 5AL
General Welsh football

The Ugly Inside
6 Dimond Close, Bitterne Park,
Southampton S02 4LF
Southampton fans

Utd United
54 Chaucer Road, Herne Hill,
London SE24 0NU
West Ham United/Dundee United fans

United We Stand
8 Hartland Avenue, Urmston,
Manchester M31 1PG
Man United fans

Up
11b Aubert Park, London N5
Arsenal fans

Up Front
12 Chestnut Gardens, Stamford,
Lincs PE9 2JY
Burton Albion fans

Up'N'Under
Foxhollows, Tranby Lane, Swanland,
North Humberside HU14 3NB
General Rugby League

Up The Work Rate
134 Dickson Drive, Irvine,
Ayrshire KA12 9HD
Irvine Meadow fans

Valiants Viewpoint
47 Brabourne Crescent, Bexleyheath,
Kent DA7 5QJ
Charlton Athletic fans

View From The Tower
11 St James Grove, Poolstock,
Wigan WN3 5BX
Blackpool fans

Voice of the Beehive
Flat 2, 84 Milton Grove, Stoke
Newington, London N16
Brentford fans

Voice of the Valley
PO Box 387, London SE9 6EH
Charlton Athletic fans

Waiting For The Great Leap Forward
PO Box 2, Wishaw,
Lanarkshire ML2 8DZ
Motherwell fans

Walking Down The Halbeath Road
PO Box 6168, 11a Forth Street,
Edinburgh EH1 3LE
Dunfermline Athletic fans

Wally Lewis Is Coming
8 Lincoln Street, Wakefield,
Yorkshire WF2 0EB
Wakefield Trinity Rugby League fans

Wanderers Worldwide
62 Queensgate, Bolton, Lancashire
Bolton Wanderers fans

Watch the Bluebirds Fly
49 Nant-y-Fedw, Ynysboeth,
Abercynon, Mid Glamorgan
Cardiff City fans

Wear All Going To Wembley
27 Haddington Road, Whitley Bay,
Tyne and Wear NE25 9XE
Sunderland fans

The Web
80 Busby Road, Clarkston,
Glasgow G76 8BD
Queens Park fans

The Wee Red
Flat 4, 1 Myrtlefield Park,
Belfast BT9 6NE
Cliftonville fans

Wendy Who?
Po Box 66, Perth PH1 1YB
St Johnstone fans

Westanders
42 Hillside Close, Banstead,
Surrey SM7 1ET
Chelsea fans

The Westender
PO Box 128, Coventry CV1 5TQ
Coventry City fans

We've Won The Kop Choir Too
37 East Crescent, East Dene,
Rotherham S65 2RT
Rotherham United fans

What A Load of Cobblers
3 Stag Court, Shire Lane,
Chorleywood, Herts
Northampton Town fans

ng ball own the iddle

issue 20

tone.f.c. supporters club magazine £1

What's The Score?
PO Box 221, Liverpool L69 7DD
General Merseyside football

When The Hoodoo Comes
29 Philips Street, Bainsford,
Falkirk FK2 7JE
Dundee United fans

When Skies Are Grey
32 East Avenue, Porthmadog,
Gwynedd LL49 9EN
Everton fans

When Saturday Comes
1-11 Ironmonger Row,
London EC1V 3QM
General football

When Sunday Comes
2 Maybury Court, Shaftesbury Road,
Woking, Surrey GU22 7DT
Liverpool fans

Where's The Number on Your Back?
26 Oakwood Park Road, Southgate,
London N14 6QG
Barnet fans

Wherever You May Be
PO Box 2, Lanark, Scotland
Motherwell fans

Where Were You At The Shay?
491 Manchester Road, Bury BL9 9SH
Bury fans

TEENAGE MUTANT HERO MANCS™

The Wild Rover
113 Greenloanings, Kirkcaldy, Fife
Raith Rovers fans

Windy and Dusty
46 Ruislip Road, Greenford,
Middlesex UB6 9QL
Rotherham United fans

Win On The Plastic
PO Box 212, Preston PR2 4AF
PNE fans

Wise Men Say
Sunderland fans

Witton Wisdom
60 Highfield Road, Byfleet,
Surrey KT14 7QZ
Aston Villa fans

World Shut Your Mouth!
PO Box 408, Glasgow G21 1RY
Rangers fans

Worse Than East Fife
54 Cedric Place, Dedridge,
Livingston EH54 6JS
Partick Thistle fans

Yellow Fever
402 London Road, Aylesford,
Maidstone, Kent ME20 6DA
Maidstone United fans

Yidaho!
73 Smeaton Road, London SW18 5JJ
Wimbledon fans

York City Supporters Club Review
York City Supporters Club,
York City FC, York
York City fans

Zoot Skazine
PO Box 202, Glasgow G12 8HQ
General music/football

In a sample of about a third of this list of fanzines the Sir Norman Chester Centre For Football Research at the University of Leicester, not surprisingly, found that most fanzines were produced by young, white, middle class males.

A survey of the above list would be unlikely to disturb that vision, though the diversity of fanzines is often overlooked. They range from Jane Purdon's **Born Kicking**, the most female-oriented fanzine, through to the odd publication which borders on the homophobic and racist.

Punk fanzines in the mid-late 70s, with which the rise and rise of football fanzines is most frequently compared, were also largely confined to a particular social strata. Punk was a product of the art schools rather than the street, although it had a widespread effect in both areas of popular culture. However, what is particularly striking is the names of the fanzines...hundreds of pop culture references highlight the movement of pop into football – and football into pop.

From the moment that Mike Ticher named **When Saturday Comes** after a line from a track by The Undertones – masters of the 3-chord, late 70s, pop classics, such as the football-influenced **My Perfect Cousin** – a whole nationwide art form was spawned. Thinking up parodic and satirical titles and headings became a pastime for many soccer and music fans steeped in pop culture from the day they were born. The problem was that, as with music fanzines, this movement was responding to a visible contempt shown for 'fans' by the cultural industries themselves.

Attempts to 'reclaim the game' (as the Football Supporters Association newsletter was originally entitled) would have been better labelled 'Claim The Game' since the ball was never really theirs to play with in the first place. In an **NME** football fanzine feature in 1989 the magazine claimed:

> "Football is hip again and that's official. This is reflected on a rock'n'roll level. You've had the Barmy Army, Adrian Sherwood's Billy Bonds flexi, El's soccer anthem compilation '4-2-4' and countless articles in the weekly and monthly press. Much of the revitalisation can be explained by an older generation of kids returning to the game that they originally rejected in favour of music. However, it is a younger generation of 14 and 15 year olds who are at the cutting edge of this revival. They are the people making up the editorial boards of the hundreds of soccer fanzines that have sprung up. A few years ago they'd have been writing about their favourite rock groups, but now their energies are consumed by football prose".

As the feature also noted "in the same way that the best pop fanzines make you want to go to gigs", the best football fanzines "will have you returning to the terraces". It is this reflection of the ever-changing status of 'low art', such as popular music and football, that makes football fanzines more than an ephemeral product.

For that reason it is fanzines like **The End** and **Boy's Own**, which spawned many late 80s and early 90s club 'zines, rather than a magazine like **Foul** (disinterred in the previous chapter), that are the historical antecedents of today's fandom.

OPPOSITE
Blue Print sellers
Maine Road, April 91.

all BLISSED UP

let the carnival begin version

"I was sitting round at my mate's flat and at first we were laughing and shouting 'get in there Liverpool'. Once we realised people had died it changed. People felt they'd contributed to what happened at Heysel ..."

This quotation (which originally appeared in Pete Naylor's excellent **Sounds** retrospective on scally-dom) came from Terry Farley, a member of the **Boy's Own** collective and producer of some of the outstanding dance tracks of the late 80s and early 90s. It summarises a widespread reaction to the Heysel disaster of 1985. What is more, despite the refusal of the mass media to accept it until after Italia '90, it signals the moment of a sea-change in youth culture and football fandom across the country.

In the autumn of 1990 Labour Euro-MP, Glyn Ford, caused a considerable stir in the mass media and the European Parliament by making allegations that the racist activity of skinhead gangs at football matches was an increasing problem and that a coordinated European response was necessary.

In countries such as Holland and Germany it is certainly the case that this particular style of what the international media have dubbed 'football hooliganism' has manifested itself in recent years. In the case of what was once East Germany the skinhead styles of an ugly neo-Nazi football hooliganism have been particularly prominent. In other parts of Europe much of the activity surrounding travel to, and attendance at, football matches in the mid-late 80s and early 90s constituted a satirically accurate impression, or caricature, of 70s' British football hooligan styles.

However, despite the continued existence of racist chants and abuse at football matches in England in the 90s (and snowballing racist street violence), there is little evidence of much specifically skinhead soccer gang activity and, if anything, there is reason to be cautiously optimistic about some of the changes in English and Scottish soccer's 'style wars' over the last few seasons. What is significant, too, is that, as a result of these changes, there could be a more peaceful return to European competition for English clubs (including Liverpool) – following the five-year post-Heysel ban (excluding Liverpool) – than predicted

OPPOSITE
'Match of the Day', Happy Mondays, The Farm, Northside ... Elland Road, June 91.

75

by ill-informed press critics and government spokespersons.

Part of the reason for confusion is the continual association of skinhead style with football hooligan style, a mistaken connection made by academics and media commentators alike but not by the fans who have regularly attended British football matches over the last 20 years. British skinhead youth styles only relatively briefly coincided with football hooliganism on any mass scale: from the 1966 World Cup to the early 70s.

By then the shaven heads, Doc Marten boots, Ben Sherman check shirts, half-mast turned-up blue jeans and tight braces had all but disappeared from the football terraces and town centres because the style itself had metamorphosed into crombie and other neo-skinhead, hard-mod styles best exemplified in all the Richard Allen cult trash novels of the 70s. This popular paperback series (New English Library) spawned titles which reflected the range of styles into which skinhead had split – smoothies, sorts (girls could play too), boot-boys and inevitably, eventually, punk rock. These were recalled in an ironic, parodic fashion by Stewart Home in his late 80s reworking of the Allen tradition to historicise the rise and fall of the casuals in a pulp novel, **Pure Mania** (Polygon). Furthermore, after The Smiths' split, Morrissey, ever an obsessive pop archivist of the 60s and 70s, knowingly entitled a solo single **Suedehead** to complete the picture.

By the onset of the early 70s, too, glam rock had married together previously opposed subcultural styles: skinhead (Slade) and hippy (David Bowie, Marc Bolan and Tyrannosaurus Rex – shorn of rock's counter-cultural mystique and pomp Marc Bolan *et al* became, appropriately, just T.Rex) with pre-punk (The New York Dolls, managed by Malcolm McLaren, later to foist The Sex Pistols on us) thrown in for good measure.

Gary Glitter, glam's most tacky, and lasting, star became a cheer-leader for the terraces up and down the country from 1973, as the chorus "Come On, Come On" from the **I'm The Leader of the Gang (I Am)** chart hit rang out inadvertently on **Match of the Day** microphones and, deliberately, as the preferred

soundtrack for countless TV documentaries on football and its hooligan problem long after even punk had come and gone.

The Bay City Rollers phenomenon in 1974, also, quickly manifested itself in terrace culture. The name of the game, even at this stage of the historical cycle, was diversity. Match days have long been a time for spotting a multitude of styles in a crowd, many of whom regarded, until relatively recently, the supposedly star professional players' hairstyles and clothing tastes as particularly naff.

When punk exploded, or rather imploded, pop culture in 1976, and briefly into 1977, the game was, in many ways, up. Heavy policing in, around, and on the way to and from British soccer matches was well and truly institutionalised. Segregation of away fans from the rest of the madding crowd gave football grounds of this period the look of a military training ground.

Punks and teds (themselves survivors from an earlier clash between soccer and youth culture in the 50s) may have fought running battles with each other in London's high streets but the English football terraces were, for once, becoming sharply politicised as the National Front, British Movement and other right-wing neo-fascist groupings sought to extend their always fragile hold on young, mainly white, working class male fans.

The response of the Anti-Nazi League was never as significant at football matches as it was on the streets or at well-attended Rock Against Racism gigs, where **Temporary Hoarding** was the precursor of many football and music fanzines of the 80s, but it undoubtedly helped to raise consciousness about the slide to the New Right which was already taking place in Britain, and elsewhere, and being consolidated by Margaret Thatcher's ascent to parliamentary power in 1979.

Skinhead gang activity, and the return of its style-leadership for many white, working class males, was evident again in the mid-late 70s. Punk bands such as Jimmy Pursey's Sham 69, which took its name from abbreviated graffiti recalling skinhead territorial gang battles in the late 60s, were constantly plagued by the crossover of skin style and neo-fascist organisations. Yet punk and skinhead figurations were often interchangeable as the politics of youth styles became ever more confused, despite the efforts of 2-Tone bands such as The Specials, The Selecter, The Beat and Madness (themselves plagued by neo-fascist hangers-on) to break down the barriers between black and white, especially in terms of musical styles.

The continued association of British skinhead style with racism and fascism manifested itself through the 80s, though rarely at, or around, football stadia. The connection was displayed first in some instances through Oi music in the early 80s and then, later, through specialist shops and low-key gigs, in a particularly nasty lyrical variant of 'hardcore' punk music which resonated in similar ventures amongst neo-Nazi skinheads in European countries like Germany.

We need to go back to the punk era to pick up the threads of youth cultural styles and football culture. But it is not punk which gives us the signpost.

By this period two significant factors were in operation. One was the continued phenomenon of 'Bowie boys' – and girls – who, under the influence of David Bowie's much-changing stage pop persona (significantly a gender-bending one which, with Divine, long predated Marilyn, Boy George, Marc Almond and others in the 80s, as did Bowie's ambivalent pronouncement of his own bisexuality) acted out numerous street performances for all to marvel at. The fan-as-star mode of youth culture had visibly come of age in the mid-70s. By the time of **Low** – with a duffel-coated Bowie on the cover – both new musical territory (the album experimented with European electronic styles which were to be influential in the 80s) and fashion style poses were breached. Bowie's crossover mass-market entrance into film in Walter Tevis' The Man Who Fell To Earth (the Nicolas Roeg film was the origin of the duffel coat and the notion of a 'postmodern' alien zapping 50 TV channels in a parody of so-called 3-minute culture) helped to solidify a casual style. A style already picking up on remnants of mod from the mid-60s as well as the fall-out from glam and the general apocalyptic mood of rip-up and wear from punk.

Casual style has had a built-in 'forever changes' mode to it: dressing up, dressing down and dressing up again in the quest for exclusivity even if it is only for a few days that, as Bowie succinctly put it, "we can be heroes".

The other important condition for the emergence of what is now referred to as casual style was Europe. The continued success of British football clubs in European competition was a crucial jumping off point (literally!) for the development of the casuals. Since Celtic's European Cup triumph against Inter-Milan in 1967 but, arguably, going back to West Ham's European Cup Winners' Cup success and Manchester United and Liverpool's stirring mid-60s performances, British clubs had provided the opportunity for their football supporters to enjoy relatively cheap travel breaks to European destinations.

By 1977, Liverpool (most prominent among the leading clubs and always in Europe competition) were going for an historic treble of League, FA and European trophies. Manchester United's unexpected 2-1 victory at Wembley courtesy of a freak winning goal (deflected in off the chest of a United player) robbed them of the chance but the unrestricted opportunities for fans travelling to and from Europe were, in the event, of more enduring significance.

Increasingly, from the 1977-78 season, which marks the official birth of the casuals as a youth culture in pop history, European shops were divested of their wares – sometimes legally, more often illegally – as brand names such as Lois, Farah, Pringle, Lacoste, Puma and Adidas and others started to take off on the terraces on a Saturday afternoon and the clubs at night.

Designer labels were ripped out, or razored off, in an ever-increasing desire to get ahead. Britain's major cities became known for rapidly-changing casual styles, their ebb and flow partially dependent on the relative success of the local football clubs and whether or not they had qualified for European competition. Liverpool's unrivalled record in this respect (stretching back to the mid-60s and forward to Heysel, after which, until 1991, they were indefinitely banned) gave Merseyside fans the best opportunity to bring back spoils of their European

conquests – scarves, jewellery, casual tops, trainers, shoes or just personal memories of bitter battles and unforgettable away victories on 'foreign' soil.

The team had also done its part on the pitch by adopting a more 'Continental' style of play (as opposed to the more traditional single-speed British model), a close, passing game which won trophy after trophy and asserted the 'pride of Merseyside' until Everton's European Cup Winners' Cup triumph shortly before the Brussels debacle.

At Heysel itself, what the Italian counterparts of Liverpool fans were wearing really mattered. The 'Juve' fans' expensive styles were a stinging reminder of the economic decline of a once-great port economy and, though there were plenty of 'traditional' football fans at Heysel, what some of the Italian 'Ultras' were sporting wasn't lost on fashion-conscious Liverpool boys. In this tale of two cities, the motto was, as always, 'if you can't beat them, look as if you can'.

The Italian 'Paninaro' look was a frequent rôle model for some aspects of casual style (especially on bands like the Pet Shop Boys) and, ultimately, much more significant an Italian influence on the football business than all the scrapbooks of Panini soccer stickers (the modernist equivalent of traditional cigarette cards) put together. 'Casual' economies in the various regions of Britain, especially Merseyside, helped build a casual style. The 'black' – or "blag" as Simon Reynolds neatly put it in excavating the Thatcherised Salford street culture roots of the Happy Mondays – economy was all that was booming in many of these places in the 80s.

Casual itself, as a label, hid sharp and obsessive regional differences over territory (place) and identity (space) in the modern world: for instance, London's chaps, Merseyside's scallies and Manchester's (Manc) perries, soon just boys or lads, reputed terrorisers of a young Morrissey in late 70s' Manchester. By the late 80s such original differences had been eroded in a mass media application of scally (originally meaning streetwise youth, possibly, but not always, delinquent, a derivative of 'scallywag') to almost anyone under 21 wearing baggy T-shirts, flared jeans, sporting a floppy fringe and playing in/listening to an indie/dance band.

Casual style, though, had always represented a wicked clash of cultures; past and present concocted together in a bizarre mishmash. Subcultural theorists watched aghast as formerly understandable homologies or 'fits' (like mods and amphetamines, hippies and marijuana) were exploded in an instant: Merseyside scallies wore Pink Floyd (**Meddle** revisited?) and Bob Dylan T-shirts as fashion accompaniments to being stoned on the Anfield Kop in a carnival parade of post-punks on dope. Late 80s differences, between and within, regions also became conflated by the hysteria of media and police labelling the 'labellers'.

To some extent this narrative of casual style in the increasingly closed world of football, youth and pop culture can be documented textually. **The Face**, **Sounds**, **NME** and other artefacts from the early to mid-80s provide something of an archive but most of it (with the exception of Pete Naylor's "The World Of The End" piece for **Sounds** which never saw the light of day as takeover came) lagged woefully in the wake of the phenomenon which it was documenting (which belies the notion of blaming fan magazines themselves for the hooliganism).

Merseyside's **The End**, however, though riddled with wind-ups and false names of mythical casual football terrace (service) crews, remains the best first-hand account. As Stuart Maconie of **NME** recalls:

"At the time of The End's ascendancy the music press was in decline and there was a genuine network of underground magazines that were snapped up by eager readers as soon as they hit the record shops. There was Viz in its true infantile glory, Vague which was obsessed with Adam and the Ants, Alphabet Soup which was teenage porn from Lush members ... and finally The End. Little else was worth reading".

From the early 80s Peter Hooton (as co-editor with, originally, Phil Jones) and others produced a fanzine whose content was largely football fan-related, though it was initially billed as "The North's Finest Music Paper". By the time of its own demise in the late 80s, when football had tended to be almost completely superseded in its pages by music and fashion, it had witnessed, and helped to contribute to, the massive explosion of football fanzines in Britain and Ireland, not to mention odd examples throughout Europe.

After the era of **The End**, Hooton, whose group, The Farm, became the fanzine's best-loved band in the mid-80s justifiably cashed in on the British, and global, mass media's obsession with scally culture. This initially included mainly Manchester bands, especially the Stone Roses, Happy Mondays and Northside. Granada's midweek sport programme, which usually featured football highlights, had as its theme music Northside's **Shall We Take A Trip**, one of their songs of praise to LSD.

As Hooton rightly noted, "Mancs" would never call themselves "scallies" … but the hooked journalists took no notice. By the late 80s and early 90s, The Farm had achieved international chart success with their 'anthemic' singles **(I'm Not Your) Stepping Stone**, **Groovy Train** and **All Together Now** and a chart-busting album **Spartacus** and appeared on their favourite soap **Brookside**, one of whose characters, Sammy, had sported The Farm's T-shirts on-screen for many months in a one-girl advertising scam.

As Jane Bussmann noted in "On the Razz in Liverpool" in May 1990 supercharged scallies had changed the football and music landscape:

> "Football fever reaches clubland London's music 'n' media trendies, who until now had successfully concealed their interest in the noble pastime, now stretch nylon Juventus tops across their pallid poundage before bounding indoors for a strenuous night's backscratching. One can only pray that locker room chic will go no further".

She also emphasised the central role of The Farm:

> "The Farm are a Liverpool band whose role as figureheads and commentators of street culture with their fanzine, The End, tended to become more significant than their music. Now The End has ended, that's changed. In an intriguing collaboration, London DJ Terry Farley (Chelsea FC) himself a Farm fan and godfather of today's fanzine fraternity, has started producing their material. The result? The most raw sounding dance record in ages, 'Stepping Stone'…"

For Peter Hooton, in particular, this belated mass media interest in The Farm offered a long-desired cultural and political platform and a suitable cultural space for a retort to all those who had labelled **The End** as a magazine for hooligans. It also enabled Farm fan, Mick Jones, formerly of The Clash and Big Audio Dynamite, to cement their mutual post-punk history, to join them live on stage and even pen a tribute to the band complete with 'Ee-Aye-Ee-Aye-O' (Down on The Farm) chorus! In truth though, The Farm were always soulboys rather than punks.

Taking legitimate advantage of the band's stardom, Hooton wrote a scathing history of the 'trainer wars' in **The Face** in 1990. Under the heading "The Good, The Bad and the Ugly", he claimed that:

> "the obsession with training shoes for the youth of this country began in the late Seventies and not in the late Eighties, as some would have us believe. It came from the football terraces and the council estates of the big cities, and who gives a George Best who started it – it happened and that's a fact. In the post-punk revolution of '78/79, Adidas Samba ruled the terraces of Anfield and Goodison, quickly followed by Stan Smith's, before Puma struck back … This was real fashion, and the competition was intense. A revolution was going on that had absolutely nothing to do with the streets of Brooklyn or the Bronx. In all the years that The End magazine was printed in Liverpool, we never received a single letter about 'trainers' in America, but we did get hundreds about the training shoes the different football crews were wearing".

The Farm's rise to pop fame provoked much ink-spilling. **The Face** also documented the band's back catalogue as they belatedly, in a comprehensive article by John McCready called "Mersey Bleat" (April 1990), caught on to what had been happening on Merseyside and in and around Manchester some five years earlier.

Interest in The Farm produced dozens of **End** retrospectives. In November 1990 Liverpool University's student magazine, **Guild and City Gazette**, took a "Trip on the Groovy Train" and interviewed Keith Mullin, lead guitarist with The Farm. The article was prefaced with a frequently-cited editorial quote from **The End** in 1981:

"for too long now London and the establishment have taken lightly the threat of Scallyhood. Now the nation has been warned. The End is proof that there is new light at the end of the tunnel. Follow us and we will take over your world".

When asked about The Farm being dubbed 'The Original Scallies', Mullin argued:

"It was over five years ago ... it was just a word that was bandied around ... someone who went to football matches, robbers and that ... me grandma used to call me old fella a scally."

Hooton, himself, speaking to **NME** in 1990, agreed:

"Years ago it was true that thuggery was associated with 'Scally' but that seems to be dying out. It isn't the robbers who go to the match anymore. It's about working class culture and that's the beauty of it. It's a culture from the streets and terraces that owes nothing to the media. It hasn't been force fed to ordinary people".

Back copies of **The End** itself reflect a continuing debate about the origins of scally youth culture and a deep suspicion of academics and the media incorporating it. For instance, in Volume 6, an issue which carried the readers quiz "Are You A Scal?" answered in 30 questions, a correspondent from Crumpsall in Manchester responded to a recent (that is, April 24 1982) **NME** article on scallies:

"At long last national recognition for scallies. Although forced to live in Manchester, my origins rest in Runcorn (a true woollie) and I've been an observer of the development of this marvellous youth cult for many years. I remember the first stirrings around the time of Liverpool/Man United Charity Shield Match in 1977, the black cords, Adidas T-shirts and blue snorkels. I've been trying to explain for years to people the subtleties and intricacies of Merseyside dress sense – all I got was a bemused puzzlement".

There followed a description of styles of scally walk and tortured musings about the possible detrimental effects of the late 70s mod revival (fuelled by the release of **Quadrophenia**) on scally culture. The letter went on:

"However, my fear proved groundless as these old parkas were quickly discarded in favour of the Artic [sic] 'Biften' Jacket (with detachable hood) –

the bulkiness of this jacket emphasising the match stick like legs. The old Stanley jacket saw a revival at this stage also. As you will probably be aware the natives of Manchester have over the last two years been trying to copy the style and while reproducing it convincingly (so much so in fact I mistook several Mancs for scousers on match day in Manchester ...) it is obvious that the style is now a fashion and not a WAY OF LIFE. In my opinion the true Scals look as if he was born that way, and will never look any different – the clothes trapping may change but the actual style never does".

This letter, as with so many others during **The End's** existence, received the barbed response from Hooton and Jones, "I bet you go to University and study psychology and have got A levels in 'Scallies lifestyles syllabus C'!"

'Woollies' (woollybacks – particularly directed at Leeds United fans, but strictly 'out of town') and students received almost as much stick as southern 'dickheads' in the pages, letters and poetry corner of **The End**. London's self-styled chaps ("down here Scallies are called Chaps") occasionally wrote in but were often dismissed as 'Cockney hooligans' who couldn't read.

The letters pages of **The End** were also a testament to the violence of the so-called soccer style wars that dominated 80s football culture.

Until the mid-80s, at least, football violence by various terrace, or service, crews was highly fashionable. Correspondents to **The End** from various parts of the country delighted in marking out both the latest fashion and the scores in the recent matches between the crews. In Volume 8 in 1982 (complete with the quiz "Are You A Real Wool?" in 29 questions and fictitious interviews with amalgams of former scouse footballers 'Terry Mac Darracott' and 'Tommy Smythe') we were told:

"Blackpool are starting this season (1982-3) in bright green T-shirts, Lee Cooper stonewashed jeans and Adidas Summit (plus Black Slazies if it's cold). Preston were starting in Motorbike helmets and greasy leather jackets ..."

In another letter, "tell your scals that their glory days on the terrace and field are over", and (from a Chelsea North Stand fan):

"it seems you lot up in Liverpool are trying to get to the top of the stabbing tables. Still Mancs don't count, 200 stitches or not ... all me mates have read the End and its taken over from The Face as our favourite magazine".

Years later, by Volume 19, much of the correspondence was devoted to spotting the 'real' terrace crews and laughing at the send-ups. "The Swindon Town Kamikaze Suicide Assault Squad" wrote to proclaim that:

"altogether there are 14 of us in the firm and our ages range from 8$^1/_2$ to 37. Dresswise we're into expensive diamond pattern Pringle sweaters, skintight Lee cords, white Fila tennis socks and pricey Nike 'Vandal Supreme' sports boots, also we're well ahead in hairstyles and currently we're all into the brand new wedge style. So as you probably realise we're well ahead of the rest of the country's soccer yobs with their DA's, donkey jackets and kangaroo skin Gucci mountaineering boots."

The letter appeared next to a more believable commentary from the "Lincoln Transit Elite" who claimed to be "sporting Reebok trainers, Marc O' Polo jumpers and flat tops."

The End editorial team itself produced an article in Volume 14 under the banner headline "In Search of the Casuals" which defined the development of the various, forever-changing football styles as regional reactions to skinhead styles. In the FA Charity Shield contest between Liverpool and West Ham, **The End** argued that:

"to a man those East End 'Casuals' were a mass of boneheads, flying jackets, them beloved Lonsdale and Dr Martens ... 99% of the West Ham Casuals had Sham 69 badges".

After disposing of the claims to football fashion leadership of Chelsea, Leeds, Arsenal, Tottenham and, to a lesser extent, Manchester clubs, our faithful editors gave us an account of the "present stage of the History of Football Fashion Part 1, the sports gear":

"Firstly the reasons why 1978/79 was mentioned was because we at The End believe this was the start of the present trendy look. Those heady days of Ritzy, Fiorucci, Lois (all at sometime abused

becoming the obligatory cut-downs). When these names became played out it was decided by all to broaden one's horizons, and the cry went up Europe! Pre-season tours, unexplored territory, in other words, easy picking to be had. Hence the bringing home from the continent, of smart looking garments with strange sounding names. The situation now has got really out of hand, it's just a throw back to the three-star jumper days (the cockneys will admit they wore them around 1953!) when no group of supporters was distinguishable from another. When the likes of Oxford, even Chester have a so called trendy crew you have to say enough is enough".

Inevitably, such a summary inspired many more correspondents to deny this particular Merseyside football youth culture history lesson. For a fan from the Old Kent Road (writing in Volume 15):

"Fiorucci's were first being worn in London in '73 or was it '72 ... and in 1973 up till 1976, all teenagers were wearing Burberrys, Daks Cashmere jumpers, Fila, Italian callards and croc shoes and plenty of tom".

In Volume 16 alongside "In Search of the Casual, part 200", the story of "Johnny Casual" (the Final Word) was told by a 'novel' (story) contribution from South of Watford which acknowledged that:

"Robbin Scallie joyously points to the fifteen consecutive seasons ragging Europe. Which is all quite true, but it must be said that Lillywhites have been selling exclusive sportswear to the discerning Londoner since the days of Bertie Wooster (now there is a Casual dream)."

By the 1984-85 season **The Face** readers were told:

"Now the football season is underway there's a great difference in style between North and South. The Cockneys are still trying to buy the most expensive clothes available, while the North is wearing 21" flares with an untucked Ben Sherman shirt. Knowing the Cockneys they'll now be scouring Bond Street for Gucci flares".

This flash of a Sheffield blade runner stirred the passions of the style warriors like the fashionable Stanley knife ('We love Stanley, he's our friend' goes the refrain, and they're not recalling Stanley Matthews' dribbles) and, judging by the sheer volume of correspondence, 1985 could be seen as a year of changing north/south football fashions. "Someone who enjoys fashion" retorted to a Southern (Spurs) fan from Norwich:

> "Reading the letter about Norwich's casual scene who is 'Casual' trying to kid? Not Norwich people, that's for sure. Maybe he's just trying to influence other casuals to dress in the same stuff for another couple of years. 'Interesting to note the re-emergence of Adidas and Nike' is it? What a load of bollocks! What's interesting about training shoes, Asquacutum and Liberty? Whoopee! As far as trend and fashion is concerned, does he not think it's all 'well played out'? If Norwich is classed as a dressing backwater, he has only himself to blame. And if Lacoste is still here for another summer, I'm moving".

By this time (circa 1985) much of the argument about who wore what where, and who ran from whom, was governed by the widespread media coverage (especially in tabloid press) of the casual youth culture and its connection to football hooliganism as if it was a new phenomenon. Then came the highly-publicised events of that year at Luton Town versus Millwall, Chelsea versus Sunderland, Birmingham City versus Leeds and the horrific Heysel disaster. A new direction in football spectatorship then started to take hold culminating in the formation of an 'alternative' football fan organisation, the FSA, but fanzine culture was always much more anarchic than organised. In addition to ins/outs, bad policing, clubs' (usually bad) reaction to their fans, professional footballers' frequently laughable haircuts and clothes, **The End** had always carried pieces on popular music, politics, youth culture and fashion – all topics which have become the staple diet of the 'new' football fanzine movement.

From 1985 **Off The Ball** (now no more) and **When Saturday Comes** have helped spawn the 400-plus football fanzines in Britain and Ireland. Prior to 1985 football fanzines consisted mainly of 'one club' supporters' magazines, with the notable exception of **The End**.

By the late 80s The End's place at the forefront of the music, youth and soccer crossover had been superseded not by football fanzines in general but by the new club culture, the origins of which it had done so much to document and stimulate earlier in the decade. As one magazine writer for **20/20** put it in late 1990:

> "The End, the granddaddy of the fanzines, which had documented the rise and fall of Puma, Adidas, Gallini and Lacoste, had always covered music and its followers as much as fickle football fashions. Inspired by this, two south Londoners started Boy's Own, which has been pivotal to the terrace/fashion/ rave crossover. Its two instigators, Terry Farley and Andrew Weatherall, are now respected young dance DJ-producers, and recently returned their debt to The End's creator Peter Hooton by producing the first hits for his band The Farm".

Boy's Own is to **The End** what the 70s' **Private Eye**-lookalike **Foul!** is to the 80s/90s' **When Saturday Comes** and the best of the other modern soccer fanzines. There is a direct lineage even where the participants in the later model had not so much as read the earlier version (though writers like Kevin Sampson – later, with Suggs of Madness, manager of The Farm – contributed to both magazines and **The Face**). For instance, a **Boy's Own** issue in 1990 had the magazine's guide to "the good, sad and the ugly of the training shoe" in Top Ten form, acknowledging that:

> "since the late 70s the training shoe has been the standard footwear of the chaps. The fashion standing of a town fell or shined on what was being worn by who and when. Nowadays all manner of bods are on the trainee bandwagon – sloanes (wet-fish to you) ragas, hoolies, even plod."

However, as with the decade of difference between **Foul!** and say, **When Saturday Comes**, the times had clearly shifted between the beginning of **The End** and the later **Boy's Own** issues. From the early 80s, for instance, the widespread use of cannabis (draw) at the match and in other public places is frequently referenced in **The End** but 'old' psychedelic drugs such as LSD (acid) and new concoctions such as MDMA (Ecstasy, or E) have become equally influential. By 1990 **Boy's Own** was itself involved in a general social reaction to "excessive" indulgence in such substances, publishing an article entitled "Five good reasons why it may be preferable to just go out and get drunk instead of spending a large part of the weekend in a chemically altered state". The letters

page of the magazine expressed similar "Voices of Reason" and contained laments for the media's incorporation of a "scene" which was better "back in the old days" (that is 1987 and 1988, when the origins of **Boy's Own** itself and the Ibizan party gang was more exclusive).

In a 1991 issue a Merseyside correspondent paid a "Hillsborough tribute" to Liverpool fans, almost 100 of whom lost their lives in April 1989 as a result of the crushing at the Leppings Lane end of the ground at the start of the Liverpool versus Nottingham Forest FA Cup semi-final. Significantly, echoing the sentiments of hundreds of football fanzine articles, the letter went on to "hope no-one is at this moment thinking up sick jokes and chants about Hillsborough. We've had enough of 'Munich '58' and 'Shankly '81'".

Inevitably, regional rivalries constantly surfaced, particularly involving London, Merseyside and Manchester. By the late 80s Manchester (or even 'Madchester' to give it its most widely-used label, made famous by the Happy Mondays' **Rave On**) was seen to be part of a specialised, global image of youth and popular culture.

Phil Thornton, in the same issue of **Boy's Own** as the Hillsborough tribute, gave a long personal account of "Manchester: Centre of the Solar System" in terms of its fashion history over the last decade:

> "Some arguments will never be settled ... who invented 'Scally/Perry' dress sense? The Scals naturally claim it was they; the Mancs are equally vociferous it was they. Both agree on one thing, however – cockneys were years catching up. As an impartial observer who shops, drinks and watches footy in both cities, I'll give you my memories of this period. It's 1981 and the Scousers had started growing their fringes into wedges and wore baggy jumpers, faded Lois and Dunlop 'Green Flash' pumps. They danced to OMD ... Human League ... Kraftwerk ... and Funky disco, such as Rick James and Tom Browne. At the match, the newly-named 'Scallies' developed this Northern style of dress to encompass pastel jumbo cords, Keo and Kicker boots and every Scal's favourite garment ... the sheepy. In the wink of an eye the Mancs adopted this style themselves and as the rivalry between the two tribes is so intense, they proudly claimed that they originated

it. By 1982 the two were more or less mirror images of each other and the style spread throughout the smaller towns and cities of the Northwest. By now however the sporty foreign clobber craze had arrived from 'darn sarf' and Hurleys Golf Shop in Manchester became the mecca for the boys and girls who gladly forked out ridiculous prices for Head, Cerutti, Kappa, Fila, Lacoste and Ellesse. The Face told everyone that the type of people who wore these clothes were called 'casuals' and everyone up here laughed ... As this style remained popular amongst the working class kids around England, Manchester suddenly went into a scruffy backlash in 84. Flared jeans and cords were everywhere. This meant you didn't have to spunk £40 on a pair of trainers cos you couldn't see the fuckin things anyway. Beaten up cord suede shoes now became the big alternative to Adidas. 84 also saw the 'Snorkel craze'; everyone went frantic digging out their old school parkas ... worn loose with a polo shirt underneath and with 20" flares below ... Up until 86 you could easily tell who was and wasn't a student, but in the next year loads of scals/Perries adopted a more studentish style. Fringes got slicked back, polo necks were worn with extra baggy kecks and brogues. The scruffy but stylish Manc style of dress hasn't changed much over the years: the Happy Mondays are probably the best example of this mode ... loose gear, baggy kecks, Rizlas, beards, short hair, tide marks, spunk stains and don't-give-a-fuck attitude!"

The pages of **Boy's Own** in the late 80s are, though, a testament to a new crossover between football, pop music and youth culture which marks out a fresh terrain for the 90s, a formation that I have described as "the end-of-the-century party" – a title subsequently re-used, with my permission, by Gary Clail and the On-U Sound system for a fine *fin de siècle* album which also explored the darker side of this hedonism in hard times.

In this post-house youth culture, Eusebio (booked originally to play at **When Saturday Comes'** 50th issue party) and St Etienne, for example, were ripped out of their previous context in football mythology and placed in the popular music realm as names of 'bands' and 'artists'.

Continuing this *bricolage* the acid house/rave explosion of the late 80s celebrated the rise of the DJ/

producer/remixer – like Andy Weatherall, Paul Oakenfold (remixer of Gary Clail's hit **Human Nature**) and Terry Farley, all associated with **Boy's Own** – as if they were football players or teams ... literally, in terms of the ecstatic cheering of fans. On the other hand, bands like Paris Angels were street/terrace fashion models getting up on stage.

Peter Hooton, when asked in **Melody Maker** in 1990 if he agreed that the decrease in the amount of violence at soccer matches over the last couple of seasons was a direct result of Acid House, replied,

> "Yeah, I'd say that's definitely true ... A couple of years ago there'd have been a really bad atmosphere between groups of lads from Liverpool, Manchester, London, this city, that city, but that's unthinkable now".

As if to symbolise this point The Farm were billed with Happy Mondays, Northside, The La's and The High to play a concert in June 1991 at Leeds United's football ground, Elland Road, beloved of television commentators for its 'atmosphere'.

In the late 80s and early 90s the football terraces, then, experienced their own 'summer of love'. The carnivalesque – even surrealist – nature of this transformation in football culture was first indicated by the inflatables craze started by Man City fans and their blown up bananas, and speedily followed by virtually every other club's supporters.

The 1988-89 season 'bananamania' inflatables ranged from Oldham Athletic's Yard Dogs (an ironic retort to a comment from ex-manager Jimmy Frizzell) through Stoke City's Pink Panthers, Bury's Black Puddings and Stockport County's Turtles to Grimsby Town's Harry The Haddocks. Stories multiplied about the origins of football's contribution to the archive of Salvador Dali modernism but, as Chelsea fan (and booker of bands at Manchester's International 1 music venue), Ric Michael, noted in **Uptown** in his regular pop culture column on football under the pseudonym 'Rictorious':

> "The craze was started by Frank Newton an exiled City fanatic who seems to be the only person connected with the craze who hasn't made money out of it. The plastic banana was a dare that Frank accepted. If he would take a friend's inflatable

banana to a City match it was his. The craze caught on, allied itself to City striker Imre 'Banana' Varadi and the rest is history; the banana mushroomed".

The phenomenon abounded and peace and mellowness reigned, helping to change the established view, so fostered by the media for 30 years, that football supporters were all hooligans. This was soccer's 'follow up to the second summer of love', the 1988 so-called Acid House or Rave craze.

News accounts still persisted with hooligan images by linking the two fields of endeavour, football and raves. "Party and Soccer Arrests Top 135" screamed a headline in a 'quality' paper after the Zenith Data Systems Cup final at Wembley in March 1990 between Chelsea and Middlesbrough at which more than 100 fans were arrested. The match occurred on the same day as "police arrested 35 people as they broke up an illegal acid house party in Cambridgeshire", where "officers came under attack from a hail of missiles after they surrounded a farm warehouse ... to prevent about a thousand people entering the building" and the two events were reported as if there was a direct, causal link.

But dance club culture was already alongside the media image of the bananarmy cult – barely understood by sports commentators – and the complex face of the 'new football fan' was being drawn. Manchester-based regional arts magazine **Avant** (now, sadly, gone) distinguished between this "new wave" fan and the "dinosaur" fan in a classic fanzine ins/outs style. **Avant** suggested that the "new wave" fan had the following photo-fit image:

> 1. long centre parting or short two-dimensional (not skin or perm).
> 2. T-shirts Baggy (club shirts/slogans/James/ Stone Roses/Happy Mondays etc) not Lacoste, Perry, Union Jack, Gazza/England/tight fit.
> 3. parallel jeans or frayed flares/tracksuit bottoms. Baggy not tight fit stonewash/drainpipes.
> 4. Puma trainers/kickers/lilac suede boots not brogues, Doc Martens, huge tongue trainers.
> 5. pin badges/bracelets/crystals not scarves/ tattoos/Rangers hats.
> 6. fanzines/obscure flags not official programmes, bricks and cans.
> 7. cannabis not beer or lager.

OPPOSITE
Everton and James fan
Goodison Park, May 91.
Everton and 'Madchester' fan,
Goodison Park, May 91.

8. other team – Cameroon not Rangers or Celtic.
9. Blue Moon/blissed up not Here We Go.

As usual this fans' guide for 'Sensually Right On Supporters' obviously had its regional base, and was underpinned by the contemporary global media concentration on Manchester and its youth culture, but it accurately reflects the changing nature of football and youth culture in England in the early 90s.

Chants like 'Blissed up' ('Oh! we're all blissed up and we're gonna win the cup ... ') and 'Blue Moon' are what mattered here not Gazza and Lindisfarne's beatbox version of **Fog On The Tyne**, or even the much more praiseworthy **World in Motion** from New Order. The singing of the words of the first few lines from **Blue Moon**, 'Blue Moon, you saw me standing alone, without a dream in my heart, without a love of my own', have produced another Maine Road 'original' (courtesy of Rodgers and Hart, 1934). Though often sung straight, the lyrics are also adapted to read 'Blue Moon, We beat United 5-1!' a reference to the 1989 Derby and, cheekily, sung in the original by Man United fans when watching the team play in their blue away strip.

Blue Print, a Man City fanzine which set about making a 'video diary' of fans in the 1991-92 season, even had master mixer Adrian Maxwell Sherwood, set it to his usual high quality Barmy Army mix, along with Granada man Clive Tyldesley's television commentary of the legendary game. **Blue Moon (the 5-1 Remix)** was born and subsequently included on a collection to publicise Sherwood's On-U Sound 'Pay It All Back Tour', a stunning 5-hour show which included just about everyone involved in the label: Gary Clail, Mark Stewart, Bim Sherman, the Maffia and Dub Syndicate, African Head Charge and Akabu. Whatever the different fans' loyalties, terrace crooning is clearly in vogue and the 'renaissance' fan is with us. If, post-Heysel, the media helped the government to (almost) kill the football industry in England in the 80s this is a remarkable celebration of fandom and the rebirth of soccer spectating ... undercutting widespread media and police predictions of violence by English fans at Italia '90.

Reports of the industry's attraction of more and more women to football grounds in the wake of the World Cup spectacle (as well as overall increase in turnstile fans) overlook a tendency, as evidenced by this chapter's archaeology of football and youth culture since the 50s, to play with traditional notions of masculinity, especially those which have been associated with football ... defence of territory, a willingness to fight ...

Women as spectators are an underresearched part of football mythology and their absence is taken for granted in much literature, but the influence of dance club culture on the terraces (and vice versa) in the late 80s and early 90s undoubtedly had already produced a 'terrace conversion' by many female fans long before the World Cup coverage. In truth, despite the live transmission and constant video replay of Italia '90, this was more of a footnote to this process though the unexpected and enlightening spectacle of an English national team playing against Germany with skill, flair and enjoyment was clearly of significance.

It is important in considering football and youth culture in England since the 50s to underline the musical representation of these changes in soccer culture.

Certainly other texts, like the many soccer fanzines, constitute a similar series of representations of the way that football and youth culture fit together historically and geographically, in terms of time and space. But football songs used to be the lowest of low art. Not any more.

Adrian Sherwood, especially, produced records in the mid-80s which were to help reorient the whole assessment of football, popular music and youth culture. Certain 12" singles produced by Sherwood became classics of their genre and, not surprisingly, much-copied in both style and substance. In particular it was Tackhead's **The Game** and Barmy Army's **Sharp as a Needle/England 2 Yugoslavia 0** which were lauded by the new football fans' heady mixture of soccer Euroclubber and vinyl junkie.

These records were heavy dancefloor mixes of sampled terrace chants and community singing, plus commentators' musings (hence the tribute to Kenny Dalglish, "sharp as a needle" as one radio commentator, Bryon Butler, put it) stolen from the television and radio. **The English Disease** (aimed at the Government's then-imminent introduction of The Football Spectators Act, 1989) featured bassist Doug Wimbish and guitarist Skip McDonald, part of the Sherwood On-U Sound 'house' troupe – some of whom also feature as an occasional On-U Sound amateur soccer team playing the likes of the **NME**. Scam promotions, run at the time by Alison Martin and Sarah Champion, author of the history of 'Madchester', **And God Created Manchester** (Wordsmith 1990), neatly summarised the significance of the record in the context of publicity material for the album:

> "Football records are by and large limited by the fact that they appeal to the supporters of a particular club, or occasionally a hilarious 'boys in the bath' type ditty by a national team. There have been some wonderful match commentary/atmosphere LP's and some recent albums have attempted to compile the best/worst of club 'footie' songs. The Barmy Army present a collection of songs that celebrate England's national game and hopefully encompass the best of the previous laughable attempts. While also equally amusing The English Disease is a serious shot; rhythms of the highest calibre. By utilising up to date techniques, skill and flair, The Barmy Army and a dribbling Adrian Sherwood have produced a winner. A verbal volley is unleashed at the government's Football Spectators Bill. Brian Clough gets 'physically involved'. 'Leroy, Leroy' chant West Ham's supporters. There's a tribute to King Kenny (Dalglish) and the North-South divide is narrowed in 'Mind The Gap'".

Apart from critical comments on the sleeve of the album, **NME**'s record review by Danny Kelly could almost have substituted as publicity blurb. It argued that:

> "Adrian Sherwood is a genius ... He has combined the second most beautiful, precious and important thing on the planet (the extraordinary meshes of gnarled noise and fluid funk that's been his trademark this last half decade) and thrillingly combined it with the first, football ... Sherwood understands that human speech, chanting, commentaries, everything, has a rhythm of its own and he's the complete master of matching rhythms and sounds. making

them inseparable, and their combination inspired".

As a result of Adrian Sherwood's miraculous efforts, new concoctions of terrace chants, commentary, interviews and cheering began to echo around the nation's dancefloors in a constant circulation, deconstruction, then reconstruction, of various contemporary elements of football, popular music and pop culture. It is not surprising that football chants have been seized on so avidly. In many ways it is football terrace culture which has the last remaining 'folk songs', passed on by word of mouth, and sampled for the fanzine flexi disc.

This soccer/music crossover is by no means confined to Britain.

Following in the post-punk mould, and uncompromising footsteps, of Mark E. Smith and The Fall (whose **Kicker Conspiracy** video was recorded at Burnley's Turf Moor ground), Cor Gout's Dutch underground cabaret-rock band, Trespassers W, (assisted on some recorded work by England, Brighton and Albanian football fan and singer/songwriter Attila The Stockbroker), released a double album, **Dummy,** in 1988 on their own TW label. Complete with a sleeve and 24-page lyric/art booklet which is adorned with elementary drawings of soccer players, **Dummy** depicts a postmodern world on the brink of madness using soccer as a metaphor.

The title is derived from a football manoeuvre, the dummy pass, which is indeed what is illustrated on the sleeve, and the whole enterprise is dedicated to Faas Wilkes who was, from the inter-war years, "the best Dutch dummy passer ever". Moreover, Cor Gout's regular Dutch language cultural politics magazine, **Mondain den Haag**, which supplements the activities of Trespassers W as a band, features articles on anything from French cultural theory to British football fanzines.

In the 80s and 90s one of the best examples of the soccer and pop music culture mix, plus a large dose of terrace narcissism, is the Italian monthly, **Supertifo** (Superfan), which has at least one offshoot in an almost identical Yugoslavian version.

This glossy journal, begun by Italian journalists in the mid-80s, treats football crowds with the same reverence other sports literature gives to players.

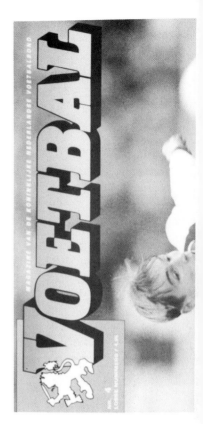

TETLEY BITTER

© IDENTITY

...AN
ON
SIXT
THE
DAY, GO
CREATED
MANCHESTER

A Leo B. Stanley Design

© IDENTITY

MANCHESTER
BORN IN THE NORTH
RETURN TO THE NORTH
EXIST IN THE NORTH
DIE IN THE NORTH

ENGLAND
A Leo B. Stanley Design

In place of, say, Klinsmann and Baggio, it highlights a colour picture of the Napoli Kop's South Boys, Hell's Rebels Battipagliese, Hooligans Teddy Boys Udinese, Bad Boys Pescara, and the rest of the Ultras at various grounds in Italy. **Supertifo** also runs small ads from people who want to swap these colour photos of 'the ends' and a chart of which kops the readers have voted the 'best'.

'Best' does not mean most violent or hooligan-oriented, despite the mistaken blanket connection of Ultras with Italian football hooligan gangs in much football literature. It means instead most colourful or the end which provides the biggest spectacle by means of scarves, showers of paper, terrace-size giant banners, team-coloured smoke flares. The fans, effectively, proclaim "We are the event".

'No Alla Violenza', the Italian fan slogan adopted, and adapted – 'No Violence Please We're Fans' – by football fans and the fashion-conscious generally around the time of Italia '90 (New Order's **World In Motion** had a **No Alla Violenza** mix done by Terry Farley and Andy Weatherall), fits into this spectrum too. However, **Supertifo**, backed by ice cream advertisers and the like, is no subversive literature – though it does explicitly deal with touchy subjects like Italian football racism – it simply picks up on the indigenous cross-connections between football and music and relies on it for its sales figures. Pop and youth culture history icons such as the Doors' singer Jim Morrison seem just as, if not more, important in its pages than the star footballers whose ubiquitous pictures adorn the other, conventional Italian sporting press. The game itself is rarely, if ever, mentioned.

Moreover, European football culture in the late 80s and early 90s was already becoming markedly different from what had gone before and such musical and youth cultural representations both reflected and constructed these changes. As Stockport County fan Richard Turner observed in his pamphlet, **In Your Blood**:

> "The terraces have also provided a showground for many of the youth cults from the 50s onwards, a fashion parade for mainly young males. The closest ties between these trends and football has been in the 1980s, with the soccer 'Casual' image that developed into the Acid House phenomena. Popular cultural images are an integral part of football culture, from the clothes to the chants derived from popular songs. In a society increasingly materialistic, apathetic and unimaginative, the soccer terraces provide a refuge, a chance to be someone and let off steam."

This circular movement of football into pop/pop into football – from Ben Sherman to Bim Sherman you might say – has taken another significant turn.

91

ninety minute culture

e is for england party mix

As the end of the century, indeed the end of the millennium, approaches the question of the media presentation of professional football is increasingly becoming a focus for public debate on a European-wide and global basis.

However, mention of the issue under general, blanket phrases such as 'law and orderism' or 'football hooliganism' is misleading. For example, to cite the situation in English national football culture, there is no simple connection between the emergence in the late 70s in the United Kingdom of a government of the radical, or New, Right and the changing style of governance of the social field of leisure, or cultural, industries such as soccer. This has international dimensions which cut across the political trajectories of the various nation states, though issues of regional and particular locality are inevitably raised.

The case of Italia '90 is a good example of the complexity of these questions. What is now obvious about the World Cup is that the event was a self-fulfilling prophesy ready to unwind. The story, which had a series of prefaces including previous World Cups as well as tragic events such as Heysel in 1985 and false starts such as the 1988 European Championships in West Germany, contains myriad strands.

One of those strands demands closer scrutiny: interpreting the story of football violence, especially involving English fans, at Italia '90. The reporting of this event (which hardly took place at all, despite the efforts of a small number of headcases and the immense provocation of the British government and Italian police) is a much more interwoven process than that perceived in the past.

This chapter assumes that the noticeable shift since the watershed month of May 1985 (when Birmingham, Brussels and even Bradford, in initial media accounts, became tragically entwined as instances of the so-called 'English Disease') is not simply the mass media exposure of soccer as a sport with specific social problems such as hooligan violence, but rather the marked redrawing of the boundaries of the largely private, heavily masculine world of professional football as an industry. Both economic, political and, specifically, legal regulation are involved in this

OPPOSITE
Man United fans
Amsterdam, May 91.

93

nited thugs run riot

WELCOME BACK LEEDS!

REDS of rioting Leeds fans
ned United's promotion party
Bournemouth yesterday.

ooligans hurled stones, bottles
aps of concrete at police
e the 1-0 win that clinched
e Second Division champion-

of fans were injured and six
ficers taken to hospital as the
own was turned
ttlefield.

mouth ambu-
led Roger Per-
d..." What
i defied credi-
ur crews came
ack when they
pick up the in-

mouth manag-
or Brian Tiler
lot of these
re not football
y are scum.'
ant Chief Con-
Alan Rose
"This is as bad
ng ever seen at
n in this coun-
ve never seen
like it in 33

emouth man-
ry Redknapp,
back tears.
was a disgust-
sphere. Leeds
to win the ti-
if that's their
y are welcome

Sick

I don't hear
saying how
y are to have
or such great
use that would

alarmed me
seeing people
ground that I
o were fright-
intimidated.
I was threa-
I came to the

ouble started at
when an angry

kick-off there were run-
ning battles between
police and fans.

Seven hundred
mounted police came
under heavy missile at-
tack and reacted by
charging the mindless
Leeds hooligans.

Now there are sure to
be calls for Howard Wil-
kinson's side to be
kicked out of the First
Division.

But Wilko said.
car

GOT HIM! A fan is led away by police

blasted the Football
league for not heeding
warnings.

He fumed: "I pleaded
with them to change
this fixture. We knew
that it would cause us
difficulties."

Thousands of Leeds

fans had travelled wit'
out tickets for the gan
despite pleas from p
lice, club and players

Meanwhile, Dave Ba
sett's Sheffield Unite
were celebrating afte
their 5-2 win at Leices
ter also clinched their
promotion to the Firs
Division.

Escape

But Sheffield Wedne
day were relegated int
the Second Divisio
after Luton pulled of
an amazing escape ac
at Derby.

Wednesday crashe
3-0 at home to Not
tingham Forest and Lu
ton's 3-2 win at th
Baseball ground mean
they stay up on goa
difference.

---

redefinition of the domain of the social (Margaret Thatcher claimed there was no such thing as society, only individuals) as most aspects of the football business find themselves being reshaped for the brave new era that beckons in the single European (football) market after 1992.

In England, since 1985 alone, four important pieces of what might be called football legislation have been enacted. The narratives embedded in the texts of the Sporting Events (Control of Alcohol etc) Act 1985, Public Order Act 1986, Fire Safety and Safety of Places of Sport Act 1987 and, eventually, after much controversy, the Football Spectators Act 1989, taken together with the two investigations undertaken by Mr Justice Popplewell (interim and final) and the two reports by Lord Justice Taylor on the Hillsborough disaster (interim and final), amount to a vast body of official stories about the control of soccer as a global business in the late 20th century. Further, the rhetorics of this official discourse, in the English scenario are, significantly, marked by a designation of football as disorder or as violence.

The horrific scale of the death by penning-in-cages at the Hillsborough disaster (April 15 1989) can be seen to have directly followed from a false interpretation by South Yorkshire Police that they were dealing with a violent crowd pitch invasion rather than a problem of safety and overcrowding, itself created by allowing thousands of Liverpool fans to mill around outside the Leppings Lane end of the ground. Indeed, as a result of information supplied erroneously by the police, some media stories on the day of the carnage blamed Liverpool fans for breaking into the stadium via the gate which the Taylor Report found to have been opened officially.

Lord Justice Taylor's most well-known proposal, that of introducing compulsory all-seater stadia to the whole of the country's football (as well as other sports) by the year 2000, was made, essentially, as a recommendation to improve safety for sports crowds in the wake of Hillsborough. However, David Waddington, then Home Secretary, announcing his government's acceptance of this measure, proposed it as a new panacea to combat football hooliganism, a move which has generally endeared itself to the

police responsible for implementation, who perceive it to contain manifest difficulties which nevertheless will be overcome by the redesigned ground architecture (such as more gangways between seats). It was seen, in the short term, as a direct replacement in the government's strategic armoury in its war against hooliganism for the compulsory membership (or ID) card scheme which the Football Spectators Act 1989 enshrined, but which was (though the provisions in the Act were in fact passed into law) shelved after Lord Justice Taylor had strongly criticised it on the grounds that it would make another Hillsborough disaster more, not less, likely.

Post-Hillsborough there had been renewed concentration on pitch violence at soccer matches in England. The outraged proclamations by the then Minister for Sport, Colin Moynihan, and Alan Eastwood of the Police Federation in Britain, regarding the lenient (as Alan Eastwood saw it) FA ruling on a much-publicised mass-player fracas at Highbury (November 4 1989, Arsenal v Norwich City, Barclay's League), were a prelude. Later that month Colin Moynihan called for police to arrest and charge players involved in brawls. The Guardian (November 28 1989) quoted him as saying that:

> "the police have the powers to move in and it is up to them to judge each set of circumstances. If they feel they have to use their powers, they should not hesitate. If that means arrest and charges, then so be it".

Alan Eastwood then criticised the FA disciplinary commission's decision to fine Norwich City £50,000 and Arsenal £20,000 for bringing the "game into disrepute" and said "the fine is meaningless and so is the body which decided it". He went on to say that the Minister for Sport and his office at the Department of Environment "will be as dismayed as we are by the punishment". The previous day Alan Eastwood had put forward the Police Federation suggestion of the possibility of a summons for assault in cases of on-field violence.

In the early 70s such hawkish statements would have been fodder for widespread ridicule ... in the hallowed halls of Lancaster Gate as much as in the pages of Foul, British football's sole satirical magazine of the time. The many hundreds of football fanzines of today may poke fun at such outbursts for all they are worth but it is no longer a laughing matter.

For their part the football authorities seem ultra-serious and continue to plunge headlong into the legal quagmire with government and police opinion ringing in their ears. Subsequently, Arsenal and Manchester United were fined and had League points deducted after a similar incident in the 1990-91 season.

Nowhere is the moral panic more evident than in the question of judicial pronouncements on players' behaviour on the field. It seems only a matter of time before the kind of criminal prosecution of players, undertaken in the late 80s in Glasgow after a particularly fiery 'old firm' game (involving England internationals like Woods, Butcher and Roberts) between Rangers and Celtic, becomes the norm in the football industry south of the Scottish border, creating new possibilities for judicial interpretation.

What is striking is the extent to which football and violence have become synonymous in the mass media image of football and, by extension, the international media coverage of youth culture as a whole. It is precisely this synchronicity which unfolds in the writing of the story of Italia '90.

The story of the World Cup 1990 as a gory game, rather than the 'glory game', gathered pace as Colin Moynihan, in his role as UK's Minister for Sport (and responsible for two of the competing nations, Scotland and England), lobbied for England to be included as one of the six seeded nations. Despite the confident claims of other nations, based on recent World Cup performances, England was chosen to head one of the groups. Strong denials were issued from FIFA and the Minister for Sport that any non-sporting reasons were behind the controversial decision, but suspicion persisted that the reputation of English football hooligans at home and abroad, had played some major part in the construction of criteria for decision-making.

Moynihan had already seen his own legislation, the Football Spectators Bill, pushed through Parliament in 1989 against a background of considerable disquiet from all parts of the political spectrum. Under Part 1, the Bill allowed the government to introduce a Football Membership Authority which would impose a compulsory membership scheme on all home football followers in England and Wales and, under Part 2, to ban from going abroad, on match days involving England and Wales (or their respective club sides), anyone convicted of football-related offences, as recently defined by the Public Order Act 1986, section 31.

The Bill, said Moynihan in interview in January 1989:

> "is only part of the package of measures that have been taken over a number of years... with this package of measures you have tiers of deterrence against hooliganism, none of which in their own right is the solution to the problem, but all of which add up to a package of deterrence, a package of measures to deter the hooligan element ... the problem should be addressed both inside and outside the grounds, and indeed overseas, which is why this specific Bill that we are now talking about is one additional layer of measures which in this particular case happens to relate to the specific problem inside the grounds and the overseas matches, because there is obviously a major problem still with the hooligan element travelling to overseas games as we saw in West Germany".

Despite the shelving of the identity card scheme, as a result of the Taylor Report, Part 1 of the Act remains on the statute book. It is the very vehicle for setting up the Football Licensing Authority which the Conservative government decided to use to implement the parts of the Taylor Report (such as all-seater stadia) which it provisionally accepted ... the Home Affairs Committee Report, **Policing Football Hooliganism**, notwithstanding.

Margaret Thatcher's government having strongly supported the European Union of Football Association's imposition of a severe penalty for the English role in the Heysel disaster, UEFA's long-awaited decision to readmit English clubs into European competition was seen by Colin Moynihan as dependent on the Bill's successful passage through the parliamentary process. Throughout 1989 he had repeatedly made it clear that his recommendation (*vis-à-vis* lifting the ban) to UEFA would be governed by the success or failure of the Football Spectators Bill and the visible

Totally bananas!

decline of football-related offences in England.

To this end, following disturbances in September 1989 on a cross-channel ferry to Sweden (and in Sweden itself) involving English fans en route to a World Cup qualifying match, a scheduled England friendly in Holland later that year was abandoned by the FA (whether or not on the Minister's recommendation remains unclear) for fear of hooligan clashes between Dutch and English fans.

A subsequent World Cup qualifying match in Poland, where riot police protected English fans from Polish youths' attacks, took place but the irony or significance of the incident did not seem to be appreciated in government, the media or within the football authorities more generally. A previous qualifying game in Albania had been notable for the mass media publicity given to the trouble-free trip (which even included a singing television news appearance by Attila the Stockbroker) organised for English supporters by When Saturday Comes, the best-known, internationally, English football fanzine. But the Polish game was reported more through a prism of fading Cold War rhetoric and predictions that few English spectators would brave the long distance travel to the Polish wastelands.

In the summer of 1989, as part of a coordinated strategy to, supposedly, bear down on the phenomenon of English football hooliganism, a National Football Intelligence Unit (NFIU) was set up at Scotland Yard, elevating a Greater Manchester Police Super-intendent, Adrian Appleby, to its leadership. The **Manchester Metro News** (September 15 1989) focussed on the parochial aspects of the appointment and proclaimed that the government had "given a £300,000 grant to declare war on soccer thugs". Superintendent Appleby was quoted as saying that his first task would be to target ringleaders and "hooligan generals" in all parts of the country. He said the unit would:

> "start by specifically targetting serious football hooligans and collecting information from police forces throughout the country. We will try to identify trends, such as their travel plans and the weapons they carry, then coordinate the information centrally and try to give advance warning for

matches and recommend the level of policing in and around grounds. I am certain it will be a success. Often the gangs will have junior and senior groups and the juniors will have to 'earn their spurs' before they are allowed to join the seniors. The hooligans are led by a general who contacts other groups before matches and arranges to meet. They gather in large groups but usually don't attack until there are 30 of them".

The **Manchester Evening News** (March 14 1990) featured Superintendent Appleby warning that thugs see the World Cup competition as "the apex of their football hooligan career" and predicting that up to 500 hardened hooligans from the United Kingdom would be among the several thousand expected to travel to Italy. The **MEN** article focused on the work by the Greater Manchester Police's Tactical Aid Group (TAG) which had organised dawn-raids on ten addresses in Bolton and in the Midlands.

Following closed circuit television surveillance (CCTV) at a Bolton Wanderers v Rotherham United match in February, where a "section of the Bolton crowd was filmed gesticulating and trying to intimidate Rotherham supporters", the raids of March resulted in the arrest of six Bolton supporters in their 20s and a police Superintendent's statement that "we have intelligence that some of these supporters were planning to travel to the World Cup". The article claimed that "police suspect louts from league clubs throughout the country plan to clash with Dutch hooligans during the championships" and "the suspects are being secretly monitored by police attached to the National Football Intelligence Unit".

Charged with gathering information nationally and internationally, the NFIU was the centre of preparations for policing English football fans at the World Cup finals and subsequent seasons.

The World Cup draw had been made in late 1989 and the careful preparations to isolate England on the island of Sardinia for the first round of matches had spectacularly backfired with the inclusion of Holland and the Republic of Ireland in the group. Frantically, intelligence which would help police to restrain Dutch and English fans from fighting each other in Sardinia was sought by the NFIU.

OPPOSITE
Man United fans
Rotterdam, May 91.

By March 1990 British media were reporting that the NFIU had obtained information about plans by Dutch and English football hooligans to clash in Sardinia. This was compounded by a general acceptance among police spokespersons in Britain that clashes would be inevitable, that such information and intelligence gathered by the NFIU was bound to be accurate and the best that could be hoped for would be a limit to the damage and extent of such hooliganism.

Italian police (some 60 carabinieri) were invited to observe policing of football matches in Britain around this period so that they could receive briefings from British police forces who had experience of 'the English disease'. In a reciprocal mission, police from forces such as Greater Manchester, backed by the NFIU, had themselves been scheduled for duty in June to work alongside Italian police patrolling the venues where England would play.

Malcolm George, a Greater Manchester Police Assistant Chief Constable, and secretary of the Association of Chief Police Officers (ACPO) general purposes sub-committee on hooliganism at sporting events, was reported by **Manchester Metro News** (March 16 1990) as saying that:

> "the Italian police are keen to develop a strategy which will assist the football fans to enjoy their visit to the full. They are, however, not prepared to tolerate any anti-social behaviour which interferes with the quality of life of the local people and other football spectators".

Colin Moynihan made great play of such "coordinating measures", stressing to the House of Commons in March 1990 his own role in the process by travelling to "Rome and shortly to Sardinia". He further proclaimed on national television, in the wake of the 'leaking' of the NFIU intelligence reports, that there was bound to be trouble at the World Cup and that the task of police and football authorities was indeed damage limitation determined by the best possible prior knowledge of events.

In Parliament the Shadow Minister for Sport, Denis Howell, himself a former Sports Minister, took up the theme, "The thugs of Holland and the thugs of this country are arranging their own fixtures already", he said, repeating information which had only been made available to the media by the NFIU. Mr Howell demanded that Colin Moynihan "stop the thugs leaving these shores for the World Cup", effectively repeating his long-standing criticism of the lack of toughness in Conservative government policy towards "English football hooligans".

The only counter to this general story line was provided by the Football Supporters Association (FSA), the body which formed in the mid-80s to represent football fans in Britain and to help democratise the football industry. The FSA publicity document prior to the World Cup in 1990 – faxed to the authorities in Sardinia – proudly proclaimed that:

> "The Football Supporters Association was formed in the aftermath of the Heysel disaster by a group of fans disillusioned that the national sport had lost all sense of direction. We felt that large-scale involvement by supporters in the game's decision-making process was necessary – our expertise and knowledge as customers being too valuable to ignore. Thus we aim to further the interests of fans by organising and backing campaigns on football-related issues and gaining representation on soccer's bodies. The Association has 22 branches throughout Britain, each holding regular meetings at which fans, no matter who they support, gather in a spirit of comradeship to debate and discuss the important footballing issues of the moment. These gatherings are usually attended by local and national football personalities and have helped combat the negative picture of supporters given by the sensationalist sections of the media. We believe that there is a brighter future for our game if fans demonstrate that their first loyalty is to football as a whole rather than simply their own team. Our organisation is, we think, unique because it is not centred around one particular club, rather it encompasses supporters of all teams, providing a unity which gives us strength. We are staunchly anti-racist, fully support initiatives to increase female participation in the game at all levels and believe that in the long term our methods will steadily reduce the need for crowd segregation and high police presences. Whilst we have been working hard since 1985, we really became prominent last April (1989) following the Hillsborough tragedy. We had long warned of the dangers of perimeter fencing, decaying stadia and piecemeal crowd control policies

THE *Sun*
investigates
scandal of
the pushers
who get
kids hooked
on Ecstasy

but it took the disaster to make the football authorities and government officials take our views seriously. The publication of Lord Justice Taylor's report into both the tragedy and the future of British football followed months of investigations with the FSA being fully consulted. Indeed many of our recommendations were taken on board, vindicating our strong belief that we should have been listened to earlier. The FSA now meets regularly with most of the game's ruling bodies, advises politicians on football-related matters, gives evidence at inquiries into crowd safety and disorder problems and has actively supported schemes to make clubs more conscious of their local community. The FSA is now recognised as the genuine, indeed the only, voice of fans in Britain by the government, the game's authorities, the media and the supporters themselves. We are backed by a network of independently produced supporters' publications that have grown from nothing in 1985 to projected sales of 1.5 million in 1990. Last year we presented a 400,000 signature petition to parliament against compulsory ID cards ... The World Cup provides us with an opportunity to spread news of our organisation further afield and play a vital role in improving the tainted public perception of England's football followers. Our aims centre around providing an information and advice service for law-abiding fans, marginalising the troublemakers by providing positive activities for the true football fans".

In 1991 the Home Affairs Committee Report, **Policing Football Hooliganism**, was to give the FSA even more cause for satisfaction. It read almost like an FSA document, so much of the organisation's evidence to the committee having been accepted. However, it had been the Hillsborough disaster which had brought the FSA to national prominence. Rogan Taylor, then chair of the FSA (now with the Sir Norman Chester Centre For Football Research) became a household voice as talking head after talking head revealed their ignorance of contemporary conditions for the ordinary spectator at British football grounds, or else wallowed in nostalgia for the Golden Age. Throughout 1988 Taylor had led the fight against Colin Moynihan's compulsory ID card scheme and proved himself the most telegenic, knowledgeable and articulate of all the opponents of the Bill. As he argued in December 1988, a few weeks before the Bill was published:

"We feel it is important not only to reject in principle the ID card scheme but also to make a number of suggested amendments to any Bill. If the Government is going to 'do something' about football we should urge it to include other features which directly benefit fans, such as:

1 supporters elected to club boards

2 establishment of a Football Supporters' Liaison Officer (a national 'Ombudsfan')

3 substantial rewards for deeper community involvement by clubs

4 a connected, high-profile campaign to defeat racism at football (the unmentioned face of hooliganism) ...

The essence of our objections is that the Government's plans illustrate a deep (and widely held) fundamental misunderstanding of the problem – and that its 'solution' will damage the game irreparably".

For the FSA as a whole there were several major reasons why "you should 'Just Say No' to ID cards: inconvenience, cost, danger (such as delays at turnstiles and crushing outside the ground), civil rights.

Tragically it required Hillsborough, an accident waiting to happen, as all football fans who regularly attended English grounds well knew by 1989, to make the Government perform a U-turn. By then most clubs had already introduced a form of 'voluntary' membership scheme (as the Government had insisted by threatening compulsory schemes if voluntary were not adopted) which in practice meant fans who wished to be in a particular section of the ground had to have ID cards, a requirement which remains largely in force.

The FSA campaign against ID cards was also well supplemented by a cacophony of renditions in popular song. Blammo! recorded a flexi disc wittily called **Drastic Plastic** (Rock Against ID Cards). Guy Lovelady got together a collection of speakers, singers and players who were all fans for **Bananas,** an album which included Altrincham fan Frank Sidebottom's witty ditties, Crystal Palace fans I, Ludicrous' rebel 'folk' song, **Moynihan Brings Out The Hooligan In Me,** and Brighton and Hove Albion supporter Attila The Stockbroker's torrent **Short Sharp Shock ID Card**

Merger Mania. In 1991 Attila was to return to the subject of Colin Moynihan (**Retrospective Abortion** from **Donkeys' Years 1979-199?**) berating the former Minister for Sport for not talking to the FSA.

The **Bananas'** sleeve was adorned by Man City fan (and top freelance music photographer) Kevin Cummins' pictures of inflatable-waving football fans and John Duncan's astute inscriptions. Guy Lovelady's plans to release Volume 2 of the record were, happily, scuppered when the Government announced its intention in 1990 not to use the law already on the Statute Book (the Football Spectators Act 1989).

Adrian Sherwood's Barmy Army album **The English Disease** contained **Civil Liberty** which featured Colin Moynihan's words spoken over the high-quality rhythm track, this time provided by Style Scott (from Dub Syndicate and formerly of Roots Radics), Doug Wimbish (from Tackhead), Kishi Yamamoto, Bonjo Iyabinghi Noah (from African Head Charge) and Jah Wobble. Steve Hardstaff's cover for **The English Disease** featured Subbuteo 'donkeys' in England team shirts, parodying football fans' ubiquitous "ee-aw" chant at any player regarded as less than competent in the ignoble art ... as did Attila's album cover photo and song 'tribute' to Crystal Palace, **Roll Up For The Donkey Derby**.

By summer 1990 the FSA were more confident about the justness of their cause. The FSA World Cup sub-committee, chaired by fanzine editor Steve Beauchampe, informed the media that they would be setting up their "own form of tourist information which will also be able to give out the latest on matches and ticket allocation". This alternative information and advice agency would have its own office on Sardinia which would be accessible for visiting English fans. The FSA made it clear that they saw their role as countering the propaganda about the inevitability of English football violence and that they had consciously made contacts with Italian police and the media.

In the eyes of the FSA, England's soccer supporters had already been branded as thugs by the media. Under the sensationalist headline "The Peace Squad: World Cup fans bid to thwart hooligans" which promoted the hooligan violence theme of earlier football stories, Greater Manchester FSA chair, John Tummon was quoted by the **MEN** (March 23 1990):

> "England has gained a bad reputation through the years. But some of the criticism being handed out is unfair and unfounded. This is a crucial time for our national game and we want to ensure that the World Cup goes well. There are thugs but they are vastly out-numbered by the ordinary and decent supporter. We will also have Italian speaking people with us and we intend to try to create the best possible kind of image we can. In the past some of us have felt that bad reporting by the press has actually inflamed incidents and sparked off soccer violence. We do.not want to see that happening at the World Cup".

The FSA had also been approached by the NFIU, seemingly misunderstanding the role and scope of the organisation entirely, to help in identifying 'hardcore' hooligan supporters who might be travelling to Italy, thus giving the impression, contrary to media reports, that the much-vaunted intelligence-gathering operation was proving more problematic than had been predicted.

The FSA had already campaigned earlier in the year in Manchester against soccer T-shirts on sale in the city (as elsewhere) which they thought could provoke violence at the World Cup. One showed cartoon character Fred Flintstone telling his wife 'Not Now Wilma: I'm off to Kill A Dago' on the front and, on the back, an aggressive bulldog waving the Cross of St George (an adopted symbol for ultra right neo-fascist organisations) with the legend 'Italy 1990: Lock Up Your Daughters'. Another had the Cross of St George replaced by a Man United flag with the boast 'These Colours Don't Run' underneath.

John Tummon argued in the **MEN** (January 3 1990) that they were "a threat to public order" and Pauline Whitby, then chair of the Greater Manchester branch of the FSA, suggested that this was "the last thing we need when all eyes will be on England supporters". In the same article an FA spokesperson was quoted, "these shirts are pathetic – like anyone who wears one. They are a target for violence and possibly for arrest and incitement to riot".

As a sub-text to the story of the 'England problem' the racist theme of football hooliganism was taken up

101

in British press-reporting of what were seen to be increases in soccer hooliganism in Italy itself during the season immediately prior to the World Cup. **The Guardian** (March 6 1990) referred to an incident in Florence where:

> "masked soccer hooligans, armed with baseball bats, beat up a Tunisian during all-night carnival facilities on Shrove Tuesday ... Police have identified the baseball attacker [sic] from his record of brawls at the football stadium. Since he is still a few weeks away from his 18th birthday he has not been detained and says he will do it again".

How do we interpret the story of the English-inspired football violence at the World Cup in Italy?

The kind of story related here is not, of course, an isolated phenomenon. It has much in common with the process of "hyperreality" described by cultural theorists as diverse as Umberto Eco and Jean Baudrillard. Baudrillard's notion of hyperreality, the "anticipation of reality by images, the precession of images and media in relation to events" is pertinent to a football culture which is increasingly subject to global media attention. The story which has been related, and excavated, here – the writing of the event of the World Cup 1990 before it happened – is important in understanding the wider process of the production of images of 'postmodern football'.

Football with Attitude began with a cautionary tale about believing what is written in football books. The intervening pages are much more a 'book about football': if it has made its mark it should have read like a live game on TV rather than pre-recorded highlights. Its peaks and troughs represent the 90 minutes (plus extra time in cup matches) of play – thrills, spills and bellylaughs plus long periods of watching the fans because the numbing activity on the field drives you to distraction.

The truth is that, as Fred and Judy Vermorel said about pop fans in their compulsive and compulsory books **Starlust** and **Fandemonium**, the current culture of fans is far more interesting (and more enlightening about the way popular culture is produced and consumed) than the star system. Professional soccer, more than any other aspect of the entertainment industry, is living proof of this.

Stephen Wagg's 80s contemporary social history book **The Football World** described footballers' lives in the "age of publicity" but postmodern football culture, such as it is, has hardcore fans for whom the influence of Malcolm McLaren is more important than Marshall McLuhan; Anthony H. Wilson, television linkman, Factory Records label mogul and co-owner (with New Order) of the Haçienda, stands more of a chance in the posterity stakes than Harold Wilson. They may not all be graduates of the art schools, though Jamie Reid, one-time collaborator with McLaren in the days of '76 (and, with Margi Clarke involved in Half Man Half Biscuit's comeback from the Tranmere Rovers terraces in the 90s) helped to pile on the pressure on Jimmy Hill who, as chairman of Fulham, was instrumental in threatening Craven Cottage with the big-E.

In any event the new culture of post-punk influences on football fandom continue to make their presence felt. Various 'street' styles have been widely disseminated across the nation's young football fans (and many young soccer professionals ... think of all those flat tops and savage back and sides) in a never-ending procession of phases and, as John Bale says in his book, part of the shift to a culture of postmodern football has involved the "musicalisation" of soccer. This, it could be said, is more of a 90-minute rather than a three-minute culture. 'Postmodern culture' has been seen by some cultural critics as inevitably, inexorably reactionary, seeing off past trends and processes with all the contempt for social history it can muster. But that ain't necessarily so.

Perhaps the football/pop crossover reached an inevitable peak in the 1990-91 soccer season following Italia '90. The backlash has already set in. Sneering music journalists wrote off The Farm as "ordinary" blokes making "ordinary" music while other critics take turns at foolishly rushing in to condemn every possible facet of football's links with popular music culture, though some **are** worthy of criticism.

Some prominent football fan musicians have, understandably, distanced themselves from this book ... not wanting to be prey to the mass media cavalry charge to squeeze every last drop from the news

angles on the crossover between the two cultural industries before moving, ever more avariciously, onto a new field ripe for harvesting of popular cultural images.

Bernard Sumner of Electronic, interviewed in **Melody Maker** (April 1991), explained something of the source of his disillusionment with the football industry as he had experienced it. His recording experience was, with New Order, (as well as the music for **Best and Marsh** on Granada) the production of the England World Cup theme for 1990. **World In Motion** which, with its various mixes, became the best-selling football record ever and, as journalist Ted Mico noted, has been partly "credited for reviving football's bad image". Sumner claimed that:

> "we just did the record and then they forgot about us ... They offered us tickets if England got to the semi-finals ... Wait a minute, we did get to the semi-finals. Bastards! We never even got the bloody tickets".

Part of the speeded-up media merry-go-round that Bernard Sumner and others were caught up in was the eventual, inevitable trashing of 'Manchester'. Its punters never believed 'the hype' in any case (as the 'Oldham – North of Manchester' T-shirts succinctly showed) and Liverpool, Bristol and Leeds soon experienced the selling of a provincial city to the global pop media.

But, as DJ, band manager and writer Dave Haslam rightly predicted in sharp articles in **The Face** on the rise and fall of the image of this North West city, the same media figures who built up the icon were the first to throw the stones. "Madchester" became "Badchester", almost overnight. Hyped bands like the Stone Roses spent most of the year after their excellent eponymous debut album in court – the Magistrates Court after applying some abstract art to their former record company offices and the High Court trying to get out of their early, restrictive contract deals.

One minute 'Manchester' featured in **Newsweek** global cover stories, the next **The Daily Express**, **Independent on Sunday**, **Sky TV News** and **CBS News** were excavating for angles on, as William Leith of the **Independent on Sunday** had it, "a drugs economy in recession". Leith wrote that:

> "a drug economy in recession is dangerous. With a collapsed market, the only thing to do is increase your market share. If you're a drug dealer, you get interested in guns and knives. People are worried about gang violence in Manchester. They are worried about organised crime. There is another problem though – this is disorganised crime. When criminals are organised, violence is discreet, furtive. This stuff – shootings, stabbings, people flashing guns and knives – is open. It is unsophisticated. It spills over into the public arena".

This ludicrous parody of tabloid journalism for the Sunday supplement market failed to distinguish between 'hard' drugs (like cocaine, crack, and heroin) and the amphetamine-based Ecstasy (or LSD or cannabis) and further proceeded to collapse the distinctions between their use, sale and connection with the once "booming youth culture economy". **The Daily Express** had already run stories on Ecstasy and LSD as 'hard drugs' in relation to what it saw as the "Manchester scene" and tabloid gossip about Happy Mondays' lead-singer Shaun Ryder's 'long-term heroin problem' hardly clarified matters ("Flip on to MTV and you'll find Shaun Ryder still singing about drugs", proclaimed Leith in his own up-market 'exposé'). In all this retrospective journalistic look-back-in-anguish Ecstasy was deemed as the essential ingredient. Leith wrote:

> "It is a mild hallucinogen which rids you of normal inhibitions and pumps up your sensual desires. When you take Ecstasy you want physical contact and loud noises ... Ecstasy consumed the nightclub scene. Hundreds of people took it under the same roof and danced together, revelling in the physical contact. These were kids who had grown up in the age of Aids, whose sexual identities had been formed as warning leaflets dropped through the door, as gravestones and icebergs loomed across their television sets. Ecstasy was the antidote. It was not political, like dope had been in the Sixties. Ecstasy was pure hedonism".

This deterministic view of an Ecstasy-driven youth cultural economy has some grains of truth but is completely unable to balance the 'scams' and differentiate them from the experience of those who

OPPOSITE
Man United fans
Rotterdam, May 91.

The Football Spectators Bill, 1989: An Interview with Colin Moynihan, Minister for Sport.

...ng cash or making sure that you hand something over to the ...tile operator who then has to look at it and hand it back to ...be it a ticket or even a season ticket. The technology is ...able for you to actually touch a small pad on the outside of the ... so you don't have to actually hand anything over at all, you can ...nue to walk through, touch this pad and no time is lost ...soever, and indeed potentially that could be used as a direct ...t facility, so you wouldn't even need to hand over cash whereas ...had previously done so.

...fessional football in this country seems to have been ...v in modernising its own house on all sorts of issues, ...ty, security and so on. Is this just another example of ...?

..., there are still clubs that haven't got closed circuit television in, ...ite the fact that they don't have to pay for it, as the Football ...t are paying for the installation and despite the fact that it is ...ersally agreed that a closed-circuit television camera moving ...ve the heads of a section of the crowd is a deterrent to people ...ng involved in a scrap. Even if there's no film in it, the very ...ence of that camera is a deterrent. Fortunately there *are* films ...em all and they are developing now from black and white to ...ur, which is also a great help to the police. There are still clubs ...'ve written to time and again that still haven't put it in. I regret ...ay that there are a number of clubs who are Luddite about their ...roach to tackling the problems associated with the game over ...nt years. That isn't just the hooligan problem. It is the quality of ...acilities, it's putting ladies toilets into the grounds, it's having a ...e relationship with the local community."

...at do you mean by hooligan problem because it's a ...blem which has been around for many years. How would ... characterise it?

...an be categorised in a number of ways. Undoubtedly there is a ...eral climate of aggression which is a major factor in putting off ...t of people from going to football. It is a climate of aggression ...is associated with almost a euphoric, tribal reaction that has ...n certainly affected by drink, alcohol, which seems in many ...es almost to numb normal behaviour. People get involved in a ...vd, they get carried away with euphoria, there's the chanting ...goes with that, much of it abhorrent racist chanting, and in that ...vd they lose the sense of responsibility and a very strong ...ressive instinct is fuelled by alcohol frequently and that in turn ...ally worries very large numbers of people from going anywhere ...r a football match.

...Now there is undoubtedly also the hardcore criminal element ...I think this is the area that, certainly in terms of policing of ...tball has been recognised more clearly than it was ten, fifteen ...r twenty years ago when we had the beginning of these ...blems. The 'firms' are often managed by families. The running ...em is in a very highly sophisticated, hierarchical structure. ...n the people who have started a lot of the problems have been ...ng in the comfortable seats indicating to others to start a ...vement down in the terraces. In other words, it is a highly ...eloped criminal element and the police have learned a great

were really 'living the dream'. 'Scallydelia' which quickly became a shorthand label in the late 80s and early 90s first appeared in print (as a joke) in **Bop City** fanzine but almost everyone seemed to swallow it without question.

After the latest round of media hype the drug squads of various police forces will no doubt be scouring the football terraces for Ecstasy tablets. None of this hyperpanic is new in itself; only the names have changed. In the 80s the media, eventually, caught on to the use of cannabis by fans at, and on the way to, soccer matches. Some time before Heysel one tabloid typically steamed in:

> "Lunatic England soccer fans on their way to last night's international in Luxembourg beat a booze-ban by getting stoned on drugs. They knew cross Channel ferries and coaches would be 'dry' so the bovver-boys smoked vast amounts of cannabis instead. The result – when they arrived for the big match they were as 'high' as if they were drunk. And they soon found the trouble they were looking for. Police arrested 32 England fans BEFORE the kick off ... I travelled on a Luxembourg-bound coach from London's Waterloo station – and before we reached the suburbs, cannabis cigarettes were being rolled. Joints were passed around the 50-seater bus during the 16-hour journey, and teenage boys were openly smoking the drug. The air was heavy with the smell of cannabis".

Much more of the same can be expected in the 90s, as the widespread use of soft drugs across social classes gathers pace and decriminalisation (in fact as well as in law) occurs in the New Europe as barriers and frontiers continue to come down in the wake of 1992.

Moreover, there were important aspects of a politics of hedonism which the moral righteousness of the media failed to pick up on. Now, as always, youth is synonymous with fun, as Sarah Champion emphasised in her tirade against the overtwentysomethings in **Blitz'** 100th issue (May 1991), but the context of hedonism is all important for cultural politics.

Before it decided to close its doors, temporarily, in January 1991 the Haçienda in Manchester had a long-established tradition of organising trips to Europe. The trips were run by DJs like Dave Haslam and

involved regular busing of the club faithful to venues such as Le Locomotive in Paris. With English clubs out of European competition until the 1990-91 season, it was a golden opportunity for football and club fans to 'go back into Europe'.

But this wasn't, generally, an invasion of English 'hooligans'. As Anthony Wilson argued to **Avant** (June 1990):

> "The hooligan element had ceased to be the hooligan element and had become the new hippies or whatever. That's where this new culture came from ... in Manchester ... the kids ... they've got different stuff now. No one's getting pissed anymore. They're doing soft drugs and dancing, and still going to football or whatever, but its taken the edge off the culture in many British cities".

Of course the unevenness of this sea change still matters – hooliganism hasn't disappeared, it's just been put on the backburner of fashion – but no one should ignore the signs of these (postmodern) times. Euro-clubbing has forged a new identity around the notion of 'Europe', a more tolerant, less regulated night-time economy around youth, greater pride of place to 'public', civic spaces and so on. Similarly the momentous events in Eastern Europe are being absorbed and the Little Englanders are making a noisy last stand.

Half Man Half Biscuit's passion for the East in songs like **I Was A Teenage Armchair Honved Fan, All I Want For Christmas Is My Dukla Prague Away Kit** and **1966 And All That** (liberally sprinkled with references to Ferenc Puskas of Hungary and Real Madrid and Lev Yashin of USSR) bore witness to a hidden history of European football since the 50s inculcated in British youth culture long before the breaching of the Berlin Wall. Billy Bragg (to add to his own football songs **The Few** and **God's Footballer**) sang "I had an uncle who once played/for Red Star Belgrade" in his 1991 chart hit, **Sexuality**).

But the cross-fertilisation within a wider, European youth culture by the time of Italia '90 was an even more remarkable spectacle. As **The Face** christened it, "Italia '91" followed the World Cup year in a mad scramble for Italian House records at home and partying abroad in resorts like Rimini. In footballing terms Italy may have lost the World Cup with one of the most impressive, stylish and unlucky displays in the history of the competition; however, as Dave Hill in New Statesman & Society and Karl Miller in The London Review of Books rightly pointed out at the time "Italianness" was already becoming a symbol, a complex cultural icon with far wider implications. Italy was, after all, well-known for a greater female football following and as a haven for prospective English female professional footballers bent on practising a trade banned at home despite the recent increased popularity of women's participation in the game.

This new Euro-citizenship gave birth to a different conception of nationhood, however partial. Suddenly, the Republic of Ireland was regarded as a 'home' nation. Here was a team, forged by Jack Charlton out of top English and Scottish teams, which prompted fanzine titles like Irishman Spotted Playing For Eire.

Black British players at last began to receive a serious, if grudging, acceptance after years of monkey chants off, and racist taunts on, the pitch. Such acknowledgement gave substance to Ashor Senator's reggae-style celebration in the early 80s of an all-black England team (from Alex Williams in goal to Cyrille Regis as striker) on the 12" single The Big Match (complete with Match of The Day theme). For many fans Roger Milla of Cameroon, the African continent's representative, was up there with Roberto Baggio, Lother Matthaus and Paul Gascoigne as a clear favourite as the tournament's outstanding entertainer. Inevitably a song in praise of Cameroon soon hit the reggae charts and was plundered by television eager for topical tips.

Of course, the terrain of the 'right to [an end-of-the-century] party' (appropriated even by England World Cup squad players Terry Butcher and Chris Waddle as they danced in front of fans who chanted, neanderthal-like 'Let's all have a disco') is an especially volatile one on which to fight.

'Rights' discourse is everywhere ... and usually on the Right in the 90s. But the experience of Aston Villa and Man United fans on their forays into European competition in the 1990-91 season was still salutary. The celebration in Rotterdam involving 30,000 Man United fans, following their team's victory against Barcelona in the Cup Winners' Cup, was a peaceful, joyous and generally remarkable celebration of the new soccer fan culture. The change itself seems irreversible.

In the long-term, it may mean little more than that. Just as the old national differences in styles of play are gradually being erased by the globalisation of football (giving a fresh twist to the phrase 'We are all Europeans now' for Brazilians, Argentinians and Uruguayans), so the cultures around spectatorship are undergoing a period of intensified mixing and matching.

Carnivalesque fan performances were certainly pervasive at the World Cup in 1990, from Brazil and Italy at one end to Ireland and Scotland at the other. But within months the world was plunged into ultra high-technological warfare in the Gulf where video games replaced dead bodies as the products of war. The last word to Gary Clail, Bristolian toaster for On-U Sound, from an interview with Dele Fadele in NME (April 1991):

> "The world we live in, if you put it in terms of a football game, the dark side is 3-0 up and its half-time. I can't accept that this is the way its gotta be".

boot the boot

Frances Rafferty on the problem of football hooliganism — and a possible solution that lies in better treatment of fans caged in a macho culture

VIOLENCE on, and off, the terraces is not new in football, but there is an answer to hooliganism, according to sociologist Eric Dunning.

The author of The Roots Of Football Hooliganism*, Dunning explained: "Hooliganism has a long tradition in football history, but today those involved have become much more sophisticated in their techniques and tactics as a [...] efforts to con-

ing in any kind of opportunities, that he leads during the week. The football hooligan is defending his territory and his honour. He is part of a macho culture where the tougher he is the more esteemed he is."

But if, as he suggests, this sort of behaviour is entrenched in football culture, will English teams ever be let back into Europe? "The hooligan doesn't care if his team is banned from Europe. The worse the reputation of the fans, the greater the [...] in his eyes," says Dun-

soccer vibes in the area

sound and vision

Although **Football With Attitude** documents the changes in contemporary football fandom and the emergence of the new, pop culture-influenced, football writing and the cultural conditions for it, it is also a handbook for those involved.

Hey Mister, can we have our ball back contains the most comprehensive sports fanzine list available ... though punters should always check the current **When Saturday Comes**, now selling well over 35,000 copies per month, and **The Absolute Game** for updates. The list includes all football fanzines ever produced, some of which are now defunct.

Together with the following print and sound guide, they constitute a definitive catalogue of all literature and music associated with soccer fan culture ... the tasteful and the tasteless.

Books and Articles

There is a massive international literature on football and popular culture. The following is a list of the most relevant reading for those who want to follow more closely some of the arguments presented in this book.

Jay Allan: **Bloody Casuals: Diary of a Football Hooligan** (Famedram 1989)

John Bale: **Space, Sport and the City: Football and the Urban Environment** (Routledge forthcoming)

Patrick Barclay: **From Schoolboy To Superstar** (Puffin 1983)

David Canter, Miriam Comber and David Uzzell: **Football In Its Place** (Routledge 1989)

Stuart Cosgrove: **Hampden Babylon** (Canongate 1991)

Michael Crick and David Smith: **Manchester United: Betrayal of a Legend** (Pan 1989)

Dave Cunliffe et al: **Here We Go: A Poetry Celebration of Soccer** (BB Books 1987)

Hunter Davies: **The Glory Game** (Mainstream 1985 2nd edition)

Hunter Davies: **My Life In Football** (Mainstream 1990)

Pete Davies: **All Played Out** (Heinemann 1990)

Eric Dunning, Patrick Murphy and John Williams: **Football On Trial** (Routledge 1990)

Eric Dunning, Patrick Murphy and John Williams: **The Roots of Football Hooliganism** (Routledge 1988)

OPPOSITE
Gary Clail
Manchester, April 91.
Adrian Sherwood
Manchester, April 91.

Eamon Dunphy (with Peter Ball): **Only A Game? The Diary of a Professional Footballer** (Viking 1986 2nd edition)

Fred Eyre: **Kicked Into Touch** (Senior 1981)

Fred Eyre: **Another Breath Of ...** (Senior 1982)

Nicholas Fishwick: **English Football and Society, 1913-1950** (Manchester University Press 1989)

Jimmy Guthrie (with Dave Caldwell): **Soccer Rebel: The Evolution of the Professional Footballer** (Davis Foster 1976)

John Harding: **Football Wizard: The Story of Billy Meredith** (Breedon Books 1985)

Dave Hill: **Out of his Skin: The John Barnes Phenomenon** (Faber and Faber 1989)

Arthur Hopcraft: **The Football Man: People and Passions in Soccer** (Penguin 1971, reprinted Sportspages/Simon and Schuster 1988)

John Hutchinson: **The Football Industry: The Early Years of the Professional Game** (Richard Drew 1982)

Roger Ingham et al: **Football Hooliganism: The Wider Context** (Inter-Action Imprint 1978)

Simon Inglis: **The Football Grounds of Great Britain** (Collins 1987)

Simon Inglis: **The Football Grounds of Europe** (Collins 1990)

Dan Kavanagh: **Putting The Boot In** (Penguin 1987)

Harry Lansdown and Alex Lippius (eds): **Saturday's Boys** (Collins Willow 1990)

Tony Mason: **Association Football and English Society, 1863-1915** (Harvester 1980)

Steve Redhead and Eugene McLaughlin: **Soccer's Style Wars** (New Society August 16 1985)

Anton Rippon: **Soccer: The Road To Crisis** (Moorland 1983)

David Robins: **We Hate Humans** (Penguin 1984)

Ian Taylor: **Hillsborough 15 April 1989: Some Personal Contemplations** (New Left Review 197 1989)

Richard Turner: **In Your Blood** (Working Press 1990)

Alan Tomlinson and Garry Whannel (eds): **Off The Ball** (Pluto Press 1986)

Gerhard Vinnai: **Football Mania** (Ocean Books 1973)

Stephen Wagg: **The Football World: A Contemporary Social History** (Harvester 1984)

James Walvin: **The People's Game: A Social History of English Football** (Allen Lane 1975)

James Walvin: **Football and the Decline of Britain** (Macmillan 1986)

Andrew Ward and Ian Alister: **Barnsley: A Study in Football, 1953-1959** (Crowberry 1981)

Colin Ward: **Steaming In** (Sportspages/Simon and Schuster 1989)

John Williams, Eric Dunning and Patrick Murphy: **Hooligans Abroad** (Routledge 1989, 2nd edition)

John Williams and Stephen Wagg (eds): **British Football and Social Change** (Leicester University Press 1991)

See also the excellent series of statistical football club histories by Breedon Books, Derby, and the various independently-produced club histories which can be found after long searches in the bookstores and which constitute real labours of love.

'Zines

Foul is now long since dead, but there are collections of 'golden oldies' in **The Foul Book of Football No 1: The Best of Foul, 1972-75** (Foul Publications 1976) and Mike Ticher (ed): **Foul: Best of Football's Alternative Paper, 1972-6** (Simon and Schuster 1987).

The best of the football fanzine compilations are Martin Lacey (ed): **El Tel Was A Space Alien** (Juma 1989), **Where's The Bar, the non-league version** (Juma 1990) and Phil Shaw: **Whose Game Is It Anyway?** (Argus 1989). Phil Shaw also wrote an excellent account of the importance of that other football magazine, the match programme, in **Collecting Football Programmes** (Granada 1980).

For the funniest football annuals, see **Frank Sidebottom's Fantastic Football Annual for 1990** and **Frank Sidebottom's World Cup Mexico 1990 Togger Annual** (complete with special World Cup 7" EP) both published under the imprint of one of the best football fanzines, **Rodney Rodney**. See **Offside: The When Saturday Comes Special** and **Bookable Offence: When Saturday Comes Special No 2** (Queen Anne Press/Macdonald 1990), for books from the best-selling football fanzine.

At Manchester Polytechnic, the Unit For Law and

OPPOSITE
Frank Sidebottom and Little Frank
Timperley, June 91.

Popular Culture has a collection of pop and football culture fan magazines, programmes and memorabilia which includes a public archive of at least one (in many cases lots more) of all football fanzines ever produced as well as many copies of magazines mentioned in this book such as **Mondian den Haag** and **Supertifo**.

Discs, Cassettes, CDs and Flexis:
Football-related Popular Music

On May 21 1989 I was fortunate enough to take part in a special two hour edition of Steve Barker's **On The Wire** Sunday afternoon radio programme for BBC Radio Lancashire (the best event on radio). This playlist of football-related popular music owes much to Steve's extraordinary capacity to discover a 'mix' of football and popular music, sometimes straining the link between the two industries to breaking point! Thanks to everyone else who helped to fill in the gaps in my knowledge. I am sure I have missed out some items, especially all the more 'tacky' stuff. The albums listed have many of the most cited individual tracks.

Consistent with the underlying theme of this book – football's connection to masculinity – there are hardly any women invoved in the following.

Ashor Senator: **The Big Match** (Fashion)
Attila The Stockbroker: **Ranting At The Nation** (Cherry Red)
Attila The Stockbroker: **Scornflakes** (Probe Plus)
Attila The Stockbroker: **Donkeys' Years** (Musidisc)
Barmy Army: **Sharp As A Needle/England 2 Yugoslavia 0** (On-U Sound)
Barmy Army: **Billy Bonds MBE** on Various Artistes: **Pay It All Back Vol 2** (On-U Sound) also available as a flexi with an issue of West Ham United fanzine **On The Terraces**
Barmy Army: **Leroy's Boots** available as a flexi with an issue of West Ham United fanzine **On The Terraces**; also on **The English Disease**
Barmy Army: **Blue Moon** on Various Artistes: **Pay It All Back Vol 3** (On-U Sound); also as a special On-U Sound flexi free with Man City fanzine **Blue Print** no

15 1991
Barmy Army: **Devo** on Various Artistes: **Pay It All Back Vol 3** (On-U Sound); also in a different mix on **The English Disease**
Barmy Army: **The English Disease** (On-U Sound)
Jorge Ben: **Ponte de Lanca African** on **Belez Tropical** (Sire)
Blammo!: **Drastic Plastic** (flexi, profits to "Rock Against I- D Cards")
Cockney Rejects: **I'm Forever Blowing Bubbles** (EMI)
Colourbox: **Official Colourbox World Cup Theme** (4AD)
Crucial Robbie: **Afraid To Get Kick Up** (Ariwa)
Depth Charge: **Goal** (Vinyl Solution)
The Disco Zombies: **Where Have You Been Lately Tony Hately?**
The Fans: **The Name of the Game** (Zyx Records)
Fat and Frantic: **Brian** (I'll Call You)
First Offence: **Hooligan (Monitor Mix)** (Blip); B-side of **Just Try Me**
Half Man Half Biscuit: **Back in the DHSS** (Probe Plus)
Half Man Half Biscuit: **Back in the DHSS Again** (Probe Plus)
Half Man Half Biscuit: **The Peel Sessions** (Strange Fruit)
Half Man Half Biscuit: **1966 and All That** (live version) (Probe Plus); B-side of **No Regrets**
The Hillsboro Crew (aka Heaven 17): **Steel City (Move On Up)** (Virgin)
I, Ludicrous: **Quite Extraordinary** (Kaleidoscope)
I, Ludicrous: **It's Like Everthing Else** (Kaleidoscope)
I, Ludicrous: **We Stand Around** (Rodney Rodney)
Introspec: **The Roger Rap** (rap version) b/w General Midfield and the Centre Spots; **The Roger Rap** (reggae version) (Beyond The Boundary)
The Fall: **Kicker Conspiracy** (Rough Trade)
Macka B: **Pam Pam Cameroon** (Ariwa)
New Order: **Best and Marsh** (Factory); B-side of **Round and Round**
New Order: **World In Motion** (Factory)
Pink Floyd: **Meddle** (Harvest)
Real Sounds of Africa: **Dynamos vs Caps 0-0** on **Harare** (Zimbabwe)
Real Sounds of Africa: **Tornados vs Dynamos 3-3** on **Wende Zako** (Cooking Vinyl)
Real Sounds of Africa: **Soccer Fan** (Cherry Red)

The Sect: **Summer Girl** (Damaged Goods)
Serious Drinking: **Stranger Than Tannadice** (Workers Playtime)
Sham '69: **Tell Us The Truth** (Polydor)
Frank Sidebottom: **5:9:88** (In Tape)
Sportchestra!: **101 Songs About Sport** (Agit-Prop)
Tackhead: The Game (4th and Broadway)
Trespassers W: **Dummy** (TW Records)
Trinity: **Football Match** (JA, pre)
Various Artists: **Bananas** (Rodney Rodney)
Various Artists: **Bend It**; CD only
Various Artists: **Flair 1989: The Other World of British Football** (Confection Records)
Various Artists: **4-2-4** (El Records)
Nana Vasconzalez: **Futebol** (Antilles)
The Undertones: **My Perfect Cousin** (Sire)

The 80s in Britain was a decade of numerous horrific disasters (rail, tube, ferry etc) as public services were deliberately run down and private, market 'solutions' were put in place; unfortunately singalong pop records were frequently made to raise money for the victims. Two disasters involved safety at football grounds, Valley Parade in 1985 (Bradford City) and Hillsborough in 1989 (Sheffield Wednesday). Some of the above listed records had proceeds donated to funds for such disasters. Two records were also specifically made in each case; these were, **The Crowd** (Gerry Marsden and friends): **You'll Never Walk Alone** (Spartan) and The Christians, Paul McCartney, Holly Johnson, Gerry Marsden and Stock Aitken Waterman: **Ferry Cross The Mersey** (PWL). However, the undoubted sincerity of the performers and the rightness of the cause barely compensated for the banality of the records.

Discs, Cassettes, CDs and Flexis:
Footballers' Sing-along-a-trax
Although some of the above various artists collections comprise football teams' popular music product, they do so with a certain deliberate, knowing irony – of the 'they're so bad they're good' variety. The following list is made up of the kind of music that comes under the "UK male football team vocalists"

category in the record hits statistical books published by companies like Guinness. The tracks are almost universally awful and with the exception of the **Anfield Rap** I cannot recommend – on aesthetic grounds – a single one. The criteria for inclusion in this list is merely that the record made the Top 100 UK chart. There are, and will be, many more

Arsenal FC: **Good Old Arsenal** (Pye)
Brighton and Hove Albion FC: **The Boys In The Old Brighton Blue** (Energy)
Chelsea FC: **Blue Is The Colour** (Penny Farthing)
Cockerel Chorus (aka Tottenham Hotspur FC): **Nice One Cyril** (Youngblood)
Coventry City FC: **Go For It** (Sky Blue)
England: **Back Home** (Pye)
England: **This Time (We'll Get It Right)/We'll Fly The Flag** (England)
England: **We've Got The Whole World at our Feet/When We Are Far From Home** (Columbia)
England: **All The Way** (MCA)
England: **The World Beaters Sing The World Beaters**
England: **This Time** (England)
Everton FC: **Here We Go** (Columbia)
Paul Gascoigne: **Fog On The Tyne (Revisited)** with Lindisfsarne (Best/BMG)
Paul Gascoigne: **Geordie Boys** (Best/BMG)
Paul Gascoigne (and friends): **Let's Have A Party** (Best)
Glen (Hoddle) and Chris (Waddle): **Diamond Lights** (Record Shack)
Kevin Keegan: **Head Over Heels in Love** (EMI)
Leeds United FC: **Leeds United** (Chapter One)
Liverpool FC: **We Can Do It** EP, containing **We Can Do It/ Liverpool Lou/We Shall Not Be Moved/You'll Never Walk Alone** (State)
Liverpool FC: **Liverpool** (Mean)
Liverpool FC: **Sitting On Top Of The World** (Columbia)
Liverpool FC: **Anfield Rap (Red Machine in Full Effect)** (Virgin)
Manchester United FC: **Manchester United** (Decca)
Manchester United FC: **Glory Glory Man United** (EMI)
Manchester United FC: **We All Follow Man United** (Columbia)
Nottingham Forest FC and Paper Lace: **We've Got The**

115

Whole World In Our Hands (Warner)
Scotland: **Easy Easy** (Polydor)
Scotland: **We Have a Dream** (WEA)
Scotland and Rod Stewart: **Olé, Ola (Muhler Brasileira)** (Riva)
Tottenham Hotspur FC: **Ossie's Dream (Spurs Are On Their Way To Wembley)** (Rockney)
Tottenham Hotspur FC: **Tottenham Tottenham** (Rockney)

Tottenham Hotspur FC: **Hot Shot Tottenham** (Rockney)
West Ham United FC: **I'm Forever Blowing Bubbles** (Pye)

There are countless other 'male vocalist' football tracks and the following gems of naffness, that failed to make the chart, are worth a mention:
Brian Clough and JJ Barrie: **You Can't Win 'Em All**
Peter Shilton and Ray Clemence: **Side By Side**

Steve Redhead has two compelling obsessions: football and music. He is a member of the Football Supporters Association and director of a research project at Manchester Polytechnic which seeks, among other things, to collect at least one copy of every football fanzine ever produced. He worked with Adrian Sherwood and The Barmy Army on **The English Disease** album (On-U Sound 1989-90). He is the author of **Sing When You're Winning: The Last Football Book** (Pluto Press 1987), **The End of The Century Party: Youth and Pop Towards 2000** (Manchester University Press and St Martin's Press, New York 1990) and **Unpopular Cultures** (Manchester University Press 1992).
Steve Redhead is Reader in Law and Director of the Unit for Law and Popular Culture at Manchester Polytechnic.

Richard Davis was born and raised in Birmingham ... and still managed to develop an interest in photography.
Inspired by the lively music scene he moved to Manchester in 1988 and studied Photographic Technology at Manchester Polytechnic.
Since leaving the Polytechnic Richard has joined the rising wave of exciting new photographers in the North West and has already exhibited nationally and regionally: **Bring Us the Head of David Bailey**, **This Nation's Saving Grace** and **Entertainment UK**.
Richard claims to be the second most gifted footballer in the country after Steve Bull.

... the definitive guide to Manchester music in the late
80s; energetic and evocative text by Sarah Champion
illuminated by the imaginative lens of Ian Tilton.

Published by **WORDSMITH**   **£9.99**